D1263996

JUN 11 1972

PRICES AND WAGES FREEZE

A Narrative Guide to the
Prices and Incomes Act 1966
together with the Text of the Act

The Narrative Guide by
WINSLEY SERGEANT, M.A., F.C.A.

Annotations to the Act by
E. ROYDHOUSE, LL.B.
of Gray's Inn, Barrister-at-Law

LONDON
BUTTERWORTHS
1966

ENGLAND:	BUTTERWORTH & CO. (PUBLISHERS) LTD. LONDON: 88 KINGSWAY, W.C.2.
AUSTRALIA:	BUTTERWORTH & CO. (AUSTRALIA) LTD. SYDNEY: 20 LOFTUS STREET MELBOURNE: 473 BOURKE STREET BRISBANE: 240 QUEEN STREET
CANADA:	BUTTERWORTH & CO. (CANADA), LTD. TORONTO: 1367 DANFORTH AVENUE, 6
NEW ZEALAND:	BUTTERWORTH & CO. (NEW ZEALAND) LTD. WELLINGTON: 49/51 BALLANCE STREET AUCKLAND: 35 HIGH STREET
SOUTH AFRICA:	BUTTERWORTH & CO. (SOUTH AFRICA) LTD. DURBAN: 33/35 BEACH GROVE
U.S.A.:	BUTTERWORTH INC. WASHINGTON D.C.: 7300 PEARL STREET, 20014

©

Butterworth & Co. (Publishers) Ltd.
1966

KD
2215
.S43
1966

Printed in Great Britain by R. J. Acford, Ltd., Industrial Estate, Chichester, Sussex

TABLE OF CONTENTS

Table of Contents

vi

THE PRICES AND WAGES FREEZE

1. INTRODUCTORY

1. The inflationary background.—Inflation is a disease of the body economic; one that is initially slow to develop, but which gathers speed, and which, if left unchecked, can eventually pass beyond control. The State has to intervene before this point is reached and that the Labour Government is now doing, belatedly, hurriedly but, it must sincerely be hoped, effectively.

2. Inflation is nothing new. It has been in varying degrees of evidence since money first came into use as a medium of exchange. It is now to be found everywhere: the bill has not yet been fully paid for the two major wars which played havoc with the world economy in the first half of this century. The account has still to be settled and cannot be settled painlessly. Neither deflation nor devaluation is a pleasant tasting medicine. Inflation is an insidious complaint and that is its main danger. It hurts most when it stops, though at all times it bears harshly on those who have to cope with rising prices on fixed incomes.

3. The Government's policy.—Will the Government's prices and incomes policy kill or contain inflation, or leave it rampant? That is the question; only the experience that time brings will provide the answer. The Prices and Incomes Act was hastily put together and, in its final stages, was forced through a Committee of tired men at an indecent pace. It smells strongly of politics. There are signs of panic strategy everywhere in its composition. Anomalies and obscurities abound, especially in that part of the Act which deals with overall restrictions on prices and incomes; more defects of drafting will come to light as time passes. But inflation has to be stopped: that is the overriding consideration.

4. Moreover, the Government intends to rely for the implementation of its anti-inflation policy on voluntary action. But, as the Prime Minister resolutely declared last month, it will not hesitate to act within the powers it at present enjoys and might seek additional authority if that is needed. Elaborate statutory controls over prices and incomes are at present avoided. For how long, however, can the Government depend on a sufficient acceptance of the ideas incorporated in the Prices and Incomes Act and to which employers and the unions have given only reluctant approval? How soon will the Government give the force of law to the " early-warning " system (covered by Part II

1

of the Prices and Incomes Act; see §§ 107–166), let alone the immediate prices and wages freeze (covered by Part IV; see §§ 63–88)? As will be explained these are only legally binding when they are brought into operation by Order in Council, and until then voluntary action is relied upon.

5. In judging what constitutes an increase in prices or incomes during the period of voluntary freeze or restraint there are at least three sources of guidance—the provisions of Part II, the provisions of Part IV, and the provisions of Schedule 2 (which reproduces the White Paper of July 1966, Cmnd. 3073). Once statutory provisions of Part IV are brought into operation they can be strictly interpreted on their exact wording, but until that happens it would be wise to use the three sources to illuminate each other in deciding how the Government is likely to expect the immediate voluntary freeze to apply.

6. **The position of trade union and employers' organisations.**—The Government has shown that it recognised the need to deal justly by the various interests involved. It has not altogether succeeded in giving effect to this good resolution and, for that, the fast-growing urgency of the economic situation has been partly responsible.

7. Labour relations are a very personal matter and must be tactfully and delicately handled if trouble is to be avoided. Wages are a main source of possible infection by inflation. It has therefore very wisely been arranged that the General Council of the Trades Union Congress shall be informed by affiliated unions of all pending claims. These will be examined by special committees set up for the purpose and consisting of one General Council member for each of the nineteen trade groups making up the Congress. The T.U.C. will, so as to conform with the Government's " early warning " policy, at all times tell the Government of important developments on the wages and conditions of labour front.

8. The Confederation of British Industry has, of course, its part to play and has shown an admirable restraint in its negotiations with Labour and Government. It furnishes Government with full information on claims, offers, arbitration arrangements and so on. Where national claims and settlements are concerned the Confederation, having collected all the needed information, hands it over to the Ministry of Labour. On the other hand, material available on local and company wage talks are sent direct to the Ministry. These arrangements ensure not only that justice is impartially done but that it is seen to be done.

9. **The purpose of the Prices and Incomes Act 1966.**—Every Act states its purpose in its " long title ", which is often pompous and prosy. The long title of the Prices and Incomes Act 1966 describes its purpose as being:

" to establish a National Board for Prices and Incomes, and authorise the bringing into force of provisions requiring notice of price increases, pay increases and other matters, and for enforcing a temporary standstill in prices or charges or terms and conditions of employment; in connection with recommendations made by the said Board, to amend the Restrictive Trade Practices Act 1956; to provide, for a period lasting not more than twelve months, for restricting price increases and pay increases and for other matters connected with prices and incomes; and for connected purposes."

The general purport of this declaration of purpose is fairly clear, but much of the rest of the Act is not!

10. There is however one matter of terminology which must be explained at once. The " temporary standstill " mentioned in the fourth line is not the immediate total price and wage freeze; that is covered by the later words " to provide, for a period lasting not more than twelve months, for restricting price increases and pay increases ". The price and wage freeze is however described as a " standstill " in the Government White Paper of July 1966, which is called " Prices and Incomes Standstill "*. The " temporary standstill " is the standstill while the Minister considers whether to refer a matter to the Prices and Wages Board, and while the matter is being considered by the Board. These two " standstills " are fully described in §§ 63–88, and §§ 107–166, respectively.

11. There are no sinister implications in the inclusion in the long title to the Act of such phrases as " and other matters " or " and for connected purposes ". These cover matters actually in the Act which cannot be specifically mentioned in the long title. It must, however, be admitted that these phrases helped the Government to introduce last-minute amendments, and to cover these subsequently by expanding the long title.

12. The shortcomings of the Act.—Many anomalies and many points of doubt have been left in the Prices and Incomes Act and in the White Papers which introduced the policies to which it gave effect. The Act had a rough handling in the House of Commons and in Committee Room 11; but it emerged practically unscathed. No major amendments to the Act were accepted by the Government though a number were put forward and duly discussed. The trouble with the anomalies is that they can give rise to so many different interpretations. Which of these is the correct one may not, in many cases, be decided as long as the voluntary " freeze " applies. And even if the statutory restrictions of Part IV are introduced, the matter will only come before the Courts on a prosecution or a claim for the return of an excess

---

* Now Schedule 2 to the Act (see § 29).

payment. An appeal would lie against a decision of the Courts, but there is no appeal against a report of the Prices and Incomes Board, or against a decision of a Government department, as such. The fact that the Government hope to operate the freeze on a voluntary basis does not help to clarify the position. The best advice to anybody who is uncertain of his position under this complex legislation is to apply to the appropriate Ministry, whether by letter or call. Visits to the tax inspector are generally found most helpful by taxpayers seeking a ruling, where no point of law is involved. It is to be hoped that Ministries will give equal help. The question what is the appropriate Ministry may give rise to uncertainty, but see §§ 177, 178.

2. THE WHITE PAPERS

13. Introductory.—For a thorough understanding of the purposes of the Act and of what lies behind it, a close study must be made of the White Papers which introduced the Government's policy on prices and incomes. These White Papers are Cmnd. 2577 (Machinery of Prices and Incomes), issued in February 1965, Cmnd. 2639 (Prices and Incomes Policy), issued in April 1965, Cmnd. 2808 (An "Early Warning" System), issued in November 1965, and Cmnd. 3073 (Prices and Incomes Standstill), issued in July 1966. The first and third of these are printed in the Appendix to this book. The second is obsolete (see § 17). The fourth is now Schedule 2 to the Act (see § 29).

Machinery of Prices and Incomes Policy

14. National Economic Development Council.—In the first of these White Papers (Cmnd. 2577), the Government laid it down, and the T.U.C. and the employers' organisations accepted that the National Economic Development Council should keep under review the general movement of prices and of money incomes of all kinds. Goodwill will come of the Council's continued deliberations provided they are not unduly prolonged.

15. National Board for Prices and Incomes.—This White Paper also contains the Government's proposal for the setting up by Royal Warrant of a National Board for Prices and Incomes " to examine particular cases in order to advise whether or not the behaviour of prices or of wages, salaries or other money incomes is in the national interest as defined by the Government after consultation with management and unions ".

16. The task laid upon the National Board for Prices and Incomes of advising whether or not the behaviour of prices or wages, salaries or other money incomes is in the " national interest ", could prove to be very difficult. Who shall say what is the " national interest "? The

Prices and Incomes Act says that a definition has been agreed by the Government, after consultation with management and the unions. Platitudes and economic ramblings are no help to the businessman urgently seeking guidance. Nor, for that matter, is the jumble of advisory investigating Boards now littering the landscape.

Prices and Incomes Policy

17. The White Paper on Prices and Incomes Policy (Cmnd. 2639) (which was originally reproduced as Sch. 2 to the Act) dealt, in Part I, with the considerations which should, in the national interest, guide all concerned with prices and incomes, especially the National Board for Prices and Incomes, in its investigation of particular cases. The following paragraphs draw attention to some of the notable features of the White Paper. A new Schedule 2 has now been substituted (see § 29), and Part I of the White Paper can now be regarded as made obsolete by the passage of time and the development of the economic crisis. Part II of the White Paper deals with the membership, terms of reference, etc. of the National Board for Prices and Incomes and is in effect now superseded by Part I of the Act.

18. Joint Statement of Intent.—The White Paper began with a quotation from the Joint Statement of Intent on Productivity, Prices and Incomes agreed by representatives of the T.U.C. and the employers' organisations. In this statement there is solemn and official recognition that all is not well with the economy. The statement accepted that, in the present crisis, a major objective of national policy must be to ensure that British industry is " dynamic "—an overworked word these days and one that can mean many things to many men—and to make certain that its prices are really competitive. There we have one of those blinding glimpses of the obvious that are so dear to Whitehall.

19. Productivity.—It was accepted also in the Joint Statement that productivity and efficiency must be improved. Real national output could thus be raised and, at the same time, increases in wages, salaries and other forms of income would be kept in line with the rise in productivity. There was, of course, nothing new in this idea but, so far, it has been little more than a comfortable formula. Wages especially have passed beyond the boundaries thus drawn. Dividend distributions have been held in check, but largely because of falling profit margins and the need to conserve resources.

20. Price levels.—Another major objective of national policy to which prominence was given in the White Paper is to keep the general level of prices stable. Stability has not yet been reached, but all-round compulsion, distasteful though it is, could bring about what voluntary agreement has not achieved save in certain disciplined sectors of the economy. Investigations by the National Board for Prices and Incomes of applications for price increases have not, of themselves, proved to be a sufficient deterrent to the continuing spread of inflation. The Board has an overladen schedule of work and, in any case, its authority is restricted. It was set up to advise on " particular cases ", and more generally to examine references made to it from time to time by the Government, on matters of long term significance in the field of productivity, prices and incomes. "This", as Cmnd. 3073* pointed out, " will be of particular importance in preparing for the period following the standstill and period of severe restraint, when it will be essential to ensure that the growth of incomes is resumed in a manner consistent with the growth of national output." But that is a vision of a happier future. First things first; and first must come the draining away of the inflationary content of a bloated economy.

21. General considerations.—The White Paper was, in effect, an essay on the behaviour and deportment expected of all engaged in industry and commerce. It suffered from the fact that there were in it many irritating errors of omission. It failed at times to give clear explanations where these were needed. How in the absence of official guidance shall the individual decide what is right in the inevitable clash of conflicting interests? Towards its close, however, Cmnd. 2639 did give a good account of the motives backing the Government's Prices and Incomes Policy and showed a lively awareness that no economy can live in a strait-jacket. Under the comprehensive heading of " general considerations " it said " The requirement that total money income should rise in line with the growth of real national output does not mean that all forms of income should increase at the same rate. It is necessary not only to create the conditions in which essential structural readjustments can be carried out smoothly but also to *promote social justice* ". The italics are ours; this reference to " social justice " clearly had in mind the Government's frequent reference in recent pronouncements to the " national interest ": " social justice " and the " national interest " are much the same concept. But neither is easy to measure.

22. The general review of money incomes of all kinds undertaken by the National Economic Development Council will, concluded Cmnd. 2639, call for the putting together of facts about the movement of the main categories of income—wages, salaries, income from self-employment, profits (distributed and undistributed) and rent. It will require also, an appraisal of the way distribution of the national income is developing under the impact of the Government's prices and incomes policy. Then Cmnd. 2639 closed with this warning: "The Government

---

* Now Schedule 2 to the Act (see § 29).

have pledged themselves to use their fiscal powers or other appropriate means to correct excessive growth in aggregate profits as compared with the growth of total wages and salaries, after allowing for short-term fluctuations."

23. So said the Government as far back as April 1965, emphasising that the making of excessive profit would not be tolerated, and threatening that the tax-weapon would be used, if need be, to prevent it. This was the Government's own " early warning ". Of course, the same weapon could be employed to deter dividend increases. But, again, a question mark rears up. Profit and profit margins differ as between trade and trade and company and company. Companies that have recently spent heavily on machinery and plant modernisation and on the erection of new buildings have now less need to accumulate liquid funds and can accept lower earnings than can companies that have still important capital projects to finance. On the other hand forward looking companies are surely entitled to reward on the money they have spent to safeguard the future. There are always two sides to a question as there are to a balance sheet and profit and loss account. Some industries are obliged annually to spend large sums on research and development or each year must set aside large amounts as provision for obsolescence. Others are obliged to spend extravagantly on advertising in order to expand or even retain their markets. Nor does the Act encourage management foresight or willingness of management to take calculated risks in spite of the fact that it is on this that the level of production greatly depends. A rushed policy of curtailment equally punishes the deserving and the undeserving.

An " Early Warning " System

24. **Introduction.**—The purpose of the third White Paper, issued in November 1965 (Cmnd. 2808) is evident from its title: " Prices and Incomes Policy: An ' Early Warning ' System ". It was in September 1965 that the Government announced its intention to seek statutory power to introduce a compulsory " early warning " system for prices and incomes. This required advance notification to the Government of any intended increases in prices or charges, of claims relating to pay, hours or other major improvements and of prospective terms of settlement in such cases. The idea was discussed with the T.U.C. and the Confederation of British Industry and earned their approval. It was, indeed, a necessary prelude to full scale legislation and was meant to give the Government time to look thoroughly into decisions on prices and pay before they were put into effect. Unfortunately, though " early-warning " was intended to avoid the possibility of hurried, last-minute legislation, it did not do so. Early action was what was really needed.

25. **List of goods subject to early-warning system.**—Not all consumer

goods and services were included in the White Paper's list of goods and services subject to " early warning ": in general only goods of special economic importance came in, or consumer goods which were an important constituent of the cost of living index. A criticised feature of this list—it is luckily provisional—was that it brings an odd assortment of Government departments into the picture. Included in the list were the Ministry of Agriculture, Fisheries and Food, the Board of Trade, the Ministry of Technology, the Ministry of Public Buildings and Works and the Ministry of Power; an " old Uncle Tom Cobley and all " arrangement that could cause confusion and delay. In view, however, of the many interests involved, it is hard to see how that can be avoided. In July 1966 the Government announced (see § 31) that the list of goods was to be extended.

26. **Food prices.**—Food prices are, of course, prominent in the " early warning " list and the products specially selected represent rather more than one-half of total consumer outlay on food and drink. Some foodstuffs were already subject to a round-the-clock inspection by the Ministry of Agriculture, Fisheries and Food. They included mainly primary products the prices of which so depend on short-term market influences that it would be impossible to give adequate notice of price increases. Thus, in practice, the whole range of food production is now under close watch. As no system of income control could possibly work against a background of rising food prices the prominent place given in the provisional list to foodstuffs is understandable. Incidentally the prices covered are primarily those only of manufacturers catering for the home market, but, where more suitable, wholesale or retail prices may be used. Nor is it normally intended to cover prices settled by individual contract. In both instances difficulties of interpretation could cause trouble; a complaint that can be laid against the whole of the Government's Prices and Incomes Policy.

27. **Notification of price increases.**—Machinery has been devised for informing the Government departments concerned of any plans to increase prices of the listed goods and for subsequent action by those departments. The machinery can quite easily be set in motion, but a rigid timetable of action to be taken and the required very full description of the goods or services concerned could fray the tempers of over-worked staffs. The time-table is now included in Part II of the Prices and Incomes Act (see §§ 115–117).

28. **Payment and conditions of employment.**—This is a subject to which Cmnd. 2808 devoted considerable attention. In this area of control the Government can ask for information on wage claims, the progress or otherwise of negotiations and settlement terms. Information must be furnished on local and company level negotiations as well as

on negotiations having national cover so as to ensure that no group of workers is specially favoured.

Prices and Incomes Freeze

29. This White Paper (Cmnd. 3073) deals with the Government's policy on the prices and wages freeze and the way in which it is to be applied. It is to be given effect to, in the first instance, by voluntary action, but the compulsory powers in Part IV of the Prices and Incomes Act (see §§ 63–88) are in reserve. The complete freeze is intended to last until the end of December 1966, and is to be followed by a period of severe restraint for a further six months. This White Paper has now been incorporated in the Prices and Incomes Act, as Schedule 2, by an order of the Secretary of State (S.I. 1966 No. 1021), made under section 4 (2) of the Act. It therefore becomes the statement of the considerations which guide the Prices and Incomes Board on any matter referred to them. It also governs the operation of the freeze (though in this connection it has no statutory authority). It is printed as Schedule 2 on p. [*58*] of this book. A curious feature is that Schedule 2 of the Act sets out in para. 39–40 the Government's proposals for legislation which forms Part IV of the same Act.

30. Prices.—The freeze is intended to apply to all prices and charges except to the limited extent that increases may be necessary because of marked increases which cannot be absorbed in costs of imported materials, or which arise from changes in supply for seasonal or other reasons or are due to Government action, such as increased taxation. Increases may also be necessary because of increased costs over which an enterprise has not full control. The criteria for price increases are said to be more stringent than those set out in Cmnd. 2639, Part I, para. 9 (now para. 9 of Sch. 2 to the Act), while the criteria for price reductions, as set out in para. 10 thereof (now para. 10 of Sch. 2 to the Act) will apply. The White Paper points out that while the above provisions relate primarily to manufacturers' prices for the home market, wholesalers and retailers have a duty no less to do everything possible, *e.g.*, by not increasing cash margins, to avoid price increases.

31. Early warning arrangements.—These are to continue as at present during the period of freeze and severe restraint, but the Government considers it essential that they should be extended to cover a field of items wider than those listed in Cmnd. 2808, and has announced its intention of consulting the Confederation of British Industry and other interested organisations about this.

32. In the meantime the standstill applies equally to goods and services both within and outside the present early warning system, and a

---

* Now Schedule 2 to the Act (see § 29).

manufacturer who considers himself justified in proposing a price increase on any of the grounds under the heading " Prices " *supra*, should notify the appropriate department. Notification is not required in respect of increases in food prices which are under the constant watch of the Ministry of Agriculture, Fisheries and Food (see Appendix, Part B, to Cmnd. 2808), or from enterprises which are not included in the early warning arrangements and employ fewer than 100 workers.

33. Rents.—The Government is to keep under the closest scrutiny the movement of rents of private housing, although, of course, most of such rents are now within the framework of the Rent Acts. Local and new town authorities are expected in the period of the prices freeze until the end of 1966 to prevent or postpone rent increases as far as possible. The principle of the freeze is expected also to be applied to rents of business premises and of land no less than to those of goods and services.

34. Rates. Local authorities are urged to ensure all proper economies in expenditure, and so restrict rate increases.

Incomes

35. Employment incomes.—The freeze to the end of 1966 is intended, says the White Paper*, to apply to increases in pay and to reductions in working hours, but not to other conditions of service except in so far as they are likely to add significantly to labour costs. The term " increase in pay " is defined in the White Paper as including, in addition to basic pay, rates of allowance which are in the nature of pay, rates of pay for overtime and weekend working, piece rates, etc.

36. Exemptions from the freeze.—The White Paper* lists, in para. 18, a number of increases in pay to which it is not intended that the freeze should apply. It is not intended to apply to:

(*a*) Increases in payments made in compensation for expenditure incurred, *e.g.*, travel and subsistence allowances.

(*b*) Increases resulting directly from increased output, *e.g.*, piecework earnings, commissions on sales, necessary increases in overtime worked, profit-sharing schemes, etc. (Note the distinction between piece-work and overtime rates, which may *not* be increased, and piece-work and overtime earnings which may.)

(*c*) Increases genuinely resulting from promotion to work at a higher level, whether with the same or a different employer.

(*d*) Increases under normal arrangements for increasing pay with age, as with apprentices or juveniles, or by means of regular increments of specified amounts within a predetermined range or scale.

---

* Now Schedule 2 to the Act (see § 29).

37. Existing commitments.—The White Paper* points out that at the time of the Prime Minister's statement on 20th July 1966, some six million workers were expecting an increase in pay or a reduction in hours (or both) during the next twelve months as a result of long-term agreements or other types of settlement made at some time in the past. It would clearly be inequitable, the White Paper says, to introduce a freeze on incomes while allowing these existing commitments to go ahead. Accordingly, in all those cases of commitments entered into before 20th July 1966, but not implemented, the operative date should be deferred by six months, and where the original operative date was before 20th July 1966 deferment should be to a date six months later, but payment of the increase should not be made before the end of 1966. It should be noted in the above connection that section 30 of the Act (see §§ 81, 82) indemnifies an employer who withholds an increase due under a contract, and sections 31 and 32, respectively (see §§ 84, 85), allow the deferment of operation of wages councils orders and orders of the Agricultural Wages Board. But these sections do not operate until Part IV of the Act is brought into operation (see § 82).

38. New agreements.—It is not the intention of the Government that negotiations should be barred during the freeze period to the end of 1966, but no new agreements entered into after 20th July 1966 should take effect before 1st January 1967 at the earliest and they should not take effect in the following six months unless they can be justified as falling within the revised criteria referred to in para. 25 of the White Paper*, *i.e.*, criteria much more stringent than those set out in Part I of Cmnd. 2639 (see §§ 17–23); the incomes norm for this period must be regarded as zero. The guiding principle will be that of national economic and social priorities. Arbitration awards, like settlements voluntarily negotiated, will be subject to the requirements of the period of freeze and severe restraint.

39. Other forms of employment income.—It is intended that the principles of freeze and severe restraint shall apply to the many individual salaries and other forms of remuneration, including that of company directors and executives, which are fixed outside the normal process of collective bargaining. Scales of charges and fees, including professional fees, of self-employed persons are expected to be under similar restraint for the twelve months period. It may be noted that if Part IV of the Act is brought into force, there will be power, under sections 26 and 27 of that Act (§§ 68–74) to impose a freeze on professional charges as being, within the wording of those sections, " charges for the performance of services ". Such charges may also be brought within the early warning and standstill provisions of sections 7 to 11 (see §§ 112–126).

---

* Now Schedule 2 to the Act (see § 29).

40. Other money incomes.—All company distributions, including dividends, should not be increased during the twelve-month period, with the exception of distributions made to meet the special tax requirements for closely-controlled companies.

The Public Sector

41. Public services, etc.—The Government intend to apply the principles of the freeze to all prices, charges and fees of Government Departments. Employers and workers in the public services and publicly-owned undertakings are under the same obligation to act in accordance with those principles as the rest of the community.

42. Nationalised industries and statutory price-fixing bodies.—The nationalised industries are subject to the same restraints in relation to prices and incomes as the private sector, and can be made subject to the general provisions of the Prices and Incomes Act. Price-fixing bodies established by statute, such as the Transport Tribunal or the Traffic Commissioners, are expected to have regard to the principles of the freeze.

National Board for Prices and Incomes

43. Position of the Board in relation to the freeze.—The White Paper* states that the Government, the Confederation of British Industry and the Trades Union Congress attach great importance to the continuation of the work of the National Board for Prices and Incomes, both in the longer term and in the special circumstances of the freeze. The fullest use is to be made of the Board during the twelve months by referring to it proposals for prices and incomes increases for examination and report—its organisation will be adapted and strengthened as necessary.

44. Examination of longer-term issues.—The Board will also during the twelve months continue to examine references made to it from time to time by the Government on matters of longer-term significance in the fields of productivity, prices and incomes.

Proposed Statutory Powers

45. The Prices and Incomes Bill.—The remainder of the White Paper* deals with the proposals of the Government to take statutory powers of a temporary nature to control prices and wages, by the addition of a new Part to the Prices and Incomes Bill then before Parliament. This has resulted in what is now Part IV of the Act, a Part entitled " Temporary Restrictions on Prices and Incomes ". This Part is to be brought into operation by Order in Council subject to affirmative resolution, and such an Order in Council may be made at any time within a period of twelve months from 12th August 1966, when

---

* Now Schedule 2 to the Act (see § 29).

the Royal Assent was given to the Act. The Government has, however, repeatedly stated that, although they are taking these powers as a reserve measure, it is first and foremost relying on voluntary action to accomplish its purpose of a price and wage restriction.

---

3. THE INTRODUCTION OF THE BILL

46. The Bill as originally introduced into the House of Commons on 4th July 1966, consisted of Part I (the National Board for Prices and Incomes), Part II (Notices and Standstills) (*i.e.*, the early warning system), Part III (Miscellaneous matters dealing with certain price-regulating bodies and restrictive trade practices) and the then Part IV (now Part V) (dealing with matters of interpretation, expenses and the application of the Act to Northern Ireland).

47. On 14th July 1966 the Bill in the above form received a second reading in the House of Commons and was committed to Standing Committee B of that House.

48. On 20th July 1966, the Prime Minister made a statement in Parliament in which he drew attention to the fact that money incomes had been increasing at a rate faster than could be justified by increasing production, and announcing the Government's intention to introduce a freeze of prices and incomes for a period of six months followed by a further period of six months of severe restraint.

49. The next step was the issue of Cmnd. 3073 (see §§ 29–45), setting out the Government's views on the freeze provisions and its legislative proposals for enforcing them, and this was accompanied by the tabling of Government amendments to add to the Bill the clauses which now form Part IV of the Act.

50. The Committee Stage of the Bill was taken between 26th July and 4th August 1966, the Report Stage on 9th and 10th August 1966 and the Third Reading on 10th August 1966. The Bill was passed through all its stages in the House of Lords on 11th August 1966, and it received the Royal Assent on 12th August 1966.

51. Never perhaps, since World War II, has any Bill been so hurried through Committee as was the Prices and Incomes Bill. Rarely have such arbitrary methods been used to secure a Bill's acceptance. Never has a committee been submitted to an endurance test so severe as was that presided over by Mr. Harold Lever in the Committee room numbered eleven. This Committee had a membership of twenty five— fifteen Labour, ten Conservative, but no Liberals. It had to consider proposals to give the Government powers of economic coercion of a severity hitherto reserved for wartime legislation. It approved and accepted those proposals but only after long hours of toiling debate that must have left most of its members in a state of nervous exhaustion.

52. All along, the main trouble has been that the Government was caught unprepared by the speed with which the economic crisis developed, and especially by the swift tumble of sterling. Because of its unreadiness it found itself compelled, at Committee Stage, hastily to add amendments of a radical nature to a Bill already past the stage of second reading. Naturally this high-handed procedure angered the Opposition and, because of the dictatorial powers the amendments gave to the Government, caused disquiet on the left wing of Labour. A combined wage and prices freeze was not to its liking and something it had not bargained for.

53. Drama there has been in plenty. Now the Government has to make its anti-inflation policies work. These policies are fully set out in the Prices and Incomes Act, but it is Part IV of that document (Restrictions on Prices and Incomes) that most concerns most people. Businessmen and professional men, bankers, trade unionists and others should diligently search the formidable text of the Act, which is printed in this book for information and guidance.

54. No legislation has been entirely fair to all: the Prices and Incomes Act could be unfair to many in that it is a hotch potch of ideas assembled in a hurry. There has been no time to hammer it into seemly shape. It is not the main purpose of this narrative to indulge in an anomaly witch-hunt, but it is its intention to indicate some of the more obvious of the anomalies that will make the Act hard to administer and a source of grievance.

---

4. SUMMARY OF THE ACT

55. The National Board for Prices and Incomes.—Part I of the Act reconstitutes on a statutory basis the National Board for Prices and Incomes, which was originally set up by Royal Warrant on 8th April 1965, with the functions of examining and reporting on questions relating to prices and incomes referred to it and of keeping under continuous review certain specified prices or incomes. The considerations which are to guide the Board in its examination of questions of prices and incomes are now contained in the substituted version of Schedule 2 (see § 29). This Part came into force when the Act received the Royal Assent on 12th August 1966.

56. The " early warning " system.—Part II of the Act covers the " early warning " system as dealt with in Cmnd. 2808 (see §§ 24–28).

Under this Part notification is required to be given to the appropriate Minister of proposed increases in such prices and charges as are specified by the Secretary of State by order, and in pay and other claims relating to terms and conditions of employment as so specified; also of specified wage awards and settlements, and of increases in company distributions. Temporary standstills are imposed on proposed increases of particular prices or charges and on the implementation of awards and settlements for specified times or pending their examination by the National Board for Prices and Incomes. Certain penalties are prescribed in connection with price increases, implementation of awards and settlements, and failure to notify increases in company distributions. This Part of the Act is to be brought into force by Order in Council, which may bring into force all the provisions of the Part, or all of them except the provisions relating to prices and charges and company distributions, or all of them except the provisions relating to pay and other claims and awards and settlements. They may be brought into force for a period of twelve months from the date of the Order in Council, and the period may from time to time be extended by Order in Council. At any time an Order in Council may be revoked and thus bring the period to an end. As to the approval and date of operation of such an Order in Council, see § 62.

57. Miscellaneous provisions.—Part III of the Act requires certain authorities, as specified in Sch. 3, which already have statutory responsibilities for regulating prices or charges within their respective spheres, to have regard, in addition to and so far as consistent with any other matters which they may be required to take into account, the considerations set out in Schedule 2 to the Act, *i.e.*, those propounded in Cmnd. 3073 (see §§ 29–45) to which the National Board for Prices and Incomes is required under Part I to have regard. The types of prices and charges covered are transport fares, pilotage and ship dues and iron and steel product prices. This Part also exempts from the Restrictive Trade Practices Act 1956 for a limited period of time certain approved agreements and recommendations with respect to prices. It came into force when the Act received the Royal Assent on 12th August 1966.

58. Prices and wages freeze.—Part IV of the Act covers the prices and wages freeze as dealt with in Cmnd. 3073* (see §§ 29–45). Under this Part the Secretary of State is empowered to make orders directing that specified prices and charges and specified rates of remuneration are not to be increased from the date of the order without Ministerial consent, and penalties are prescribed for contravention of such a direction. Additionally, where a price or charge or a rate of remuneration

* Now Schedule 2 to the Act (see § 29).

has been increased since 20th July 1966, a Minister may direct that it be reduced to a level not lower than that obtaining before that date, and here again there are penalties for contravention. An employer who withholds from his employee an increase of remuneration falling due under a contract of employment entered into before Part IV of the Act came into force (see *infra*) does not thereby become liable in respect of a breach of contract. Increases in remuneration recommended by Wages Councils and the operation of orders under the Agricultural Wages Act 1948 fixing minimum rates of wages and holidays may be deferred. This Part of the Act is to be brought into force by Order in Council at any time within the period of twelve months from the passing of the Act (*i.e.*, 12th August 1966) and is then to operate only for the remainder of that period. (As to approval and date of operation of such an Order in Council, see § 61.) The powers under this Part therefore in any case expire with midnight of 11th/12th August 1967.

59. General provisions.—Part V covers general matters relating to interpretation, administrative expenses and the application of the Act to Northern Ireland.

60. The period of operation of the various Parts of the Act.—It will be seen from the above summary that there are three distinct planks to the Government's prices and incomes policy, which may be briefly stated as follows:

(1) Under Part I, which is permanent and has immediate effect, the reference to the National Board for Prices and Incomes of any question relating to prices, charges, wages and salaries and the keeping by the Board under continuous review of certain prices, charges and incomes.

(2) Under Part II, which is permanent, but awaits its bringing into force by Order in Council, the provision for notification of proposed increases of prices, incomes and company distributions, and of wage awards and settlements, and the standstill arrangements in relation to price and income increases and to wage awards and settlements.

(3) Under Part IV, which has a maximum duration of twelve months from 12th August 1966 and may be brought into force by Order in Council at any time during that period, the almost total prohibition on increases of specified prices, charges and incomes.

61. Approval of Orders in Council.—The Government will not hesitate to invoke the statutory powers it has been given to control wage and price levels should there be any serious departure from the principle laid down in the voluntary standstill arrangements. Parliament might have to be recalled from holiday in that case. The position under Part IV is that after the Prices and Incomes Act has received Royal Assent, an Order in Council can be made which would have immediate effect. This Order would have to be approved by Parliament within 28 days of its being made. If Parliament is normally sitting at any time during the 28 days approval could be sought then. Approval could, if desired, be sought on the same day as the order is made. If however it is not sitting during the 28 days, Parliament would have to be recalled so that the Order might be approved. Most observers of the political and industrial scenes now feel, however, that Members of Parliament will be able to take their holidays in peace and without interruption. An Order in Council made on 21st September could be approved on 18th October, the day on which Parliament is intended, under present arrangements, to re-assemble.

62. The position under Part II is different, since an Order in Council under section 6 has to be laid in draft and approved before it comes into operation. The likelihood of Parliament being recalled for this purpose is even more remote.

5. THE PRICES AND WAGES FREEZE (PART IV)

63. Operation of Part IV.—Part IV of the Act, which contains the compulsory prices and wages freeze as propounded in Cmnd. 3073* (see §§ 29–45), is undoubtedly the most controversial part of the whole Act and a potential trouble-maker. Unlike the rest of the Act, however, it is to be of only temporary operation. It expires at midnight of 11th/ 12th August 1967. The arrangements under subsection (1) of section 25 for bringing it into force have been described in § 61; its operation may be terminated at any time by a further Order in Council (section 25 (3)). Power to make orders is conferred on the Secretary of State by various provisions of Part IV, and this power may, by section 25 (2), be exercised before those provisions are brought into force as above, though they will only take effect from the date the provisions are brought into force. By section 25 (4) the lapse of the provisions of this Part at the end of twelve months or on the revocation or cessation of the Order in Council is not to affect liability for any offence committed before the lapse of the provisions.

64. The powers granted by Part IV reach far, and in any case, over the coming months, the Government must be able to move fast and to enforce its policies without delay. An economic crisis of present dimensions will not be tamed by half-hearted or tardy action. The treatment of Part IV contains many references to the White Paper of July 1966 (Cmnd. 3073) which is now Schedule 2 to the Act. Although its only statutory effect is in relation to the work of the Prices and Incomes Board (see § 104), yet it clearly governs the policy of the " freeze " provisions of Part IV.

65. Freeze problems and hardships.—The enforcement of price control has never been easy, though it is easier than control of incomes.

---

* Now Schedule 2 to the Act (see § 29).

A large administrative force has to be assembled, briefed and trained. Black markets emerge and organise an extensive under-the-counter traffic. Yet price control there must be if wage earners and the recipients of salaries, dividends and other incomes are to accept the disciplines imposed on them. Inflation can be beaten only by all-round sacrifice and, in some instances, at the cost of seeming or actual injustice. Many such instances at once come to mind and particularly in the wages field. It is here, as in regulation of dividend payments, that the fixing of an arbitrary date (20th July) for the start of the " freeze " will cause most hardship. There are as many as six million workers who will temporarily lose the benefit of salary or wage increases agreed upon before that date. The railmen, promised a $3\frac{1}{2}$ per cent. rise in September after the personal intervention of the Premier in a successful effort to avoid a rail strike, will not get their increase until next March. The seamen, on the other hand, got what they wanted before the appointed day and so are safe. The seamen escape but the doctors will suffer, as will the provincial busmen, employees of the local authorities, a number of civil servants, grocery staffs, gas workers and others. It seems unfair: it is unfair. Contracts signed and sealed have been invalidated for the time being, but a starting point has to be fixed for the coming into operation of the Government's anti-inflation measures and those on the wrong side of that point can do no more than grumble. It is proof of the nation's realisation of the nation's predicament that both employers and workers have, though reluctantly, agreed to support the Government's anti-inflation policies. Sir Maurice Laing, President of the Confederation of British Industry, has asked members of the Confederation to keep within the boundaries marked out in the prices and income standstill agreement " as fully as possible until further guidance can be given ", whilst union leaders have with reservations, made known their acceptance of the need of a wages freeze. But will the union leaders be able to control the rank and file in these next crucial months? The suggestion that para. 18 of the White Paper of July 1966* (Cmnd. 3073), which lists certain increases to which the freeze is not to apply (see § 36), should include wage increases if improved working methods resulted in increased output, was turned down. It seems hard that this list of deserving cases could not be extended to include reward for the improvement of working methods. Again, however, it must be emphasised that exemption from the restrictions laid down in Part IV and other parts of the Prices and Incomes Act must be sparingly given. This is no time for generosity.

66. Comparison between earlier and later prices and rates of wages.— There is in section 25 (7) what is in effect a timetable in relation to price and wage freezes. That subsection provides that in comparing, for the

---

* Now Schedule 2 to the Act (see § 29).

purposes of the freeze provisions, the amount of any price or charge, or the rate of any remuneration, with earlier prices or charges or remuneration paid before a specified date, so far as required for the purpose of giving effect to any order under, for example, section 26 (see §§ 68, 69) or direction under, for example, section 27 (see §§ 71–73), (*a*) account is only to be taken of such earlier prices or charges or remuneration as fell within such period before that date as the order or direction prescribes, and (*b*) as between earlier and later prices or charges or remuneration falling within that period, account is to be taken only of the later or latest. It was stated on behalf of the Government in Standing Committee that where there was a price on 20th July 1966 for any particular goods that would be the comparable base price for any subsequent comparison (see H. of C. Official Report S.C.B. cols. 461 to 474), and that should there be any case in which there was not a price identifiable on that date there should be a limitation on how far one could go back for a comparable price. In the consideration of prices the methods of comparison in section 10 (see § 124) should be borne in mind, though not strictly applicable.

Again subsection (8) provides that where a comparison is to be made between rates of remuneration for work at different times, and there are normal working hours for the work and any of the remuneration consists of remuneration for work outside those normal working hours, the order may prescribe the manner in which the comparison is to be made including adjustments which are to be made where the normal working hours are shorter at the later time. It is to be observed that this does not concern " overtime " but work outside normal working hours. In considering what constitutes an increase in pay the provisions of paras. 17 and 18 of the White Paper of July 1966* (Cmnd. 3073), outlined in §§ 35, 36, are most important and particularly the exemptions from the wages freeze.

The Act refers to " remuneration ", an expression which is nowhere defined. Does this apply only to actual salary and wages rates (including overtime rates), or does it apply also to " fringe benefits "? The White Paper of July 1966* (Cmnd. 3073) says in para. 16 that the freeze applies " to increases in pay and to reductions in working hours. It is not proposed that it should be regarded as applying to other conditions of service, *except in so far as these are likely to add significantly to labour costs* ". (Compare the notices and standstill provisions of Part II of the Act which *do* apply to other terms and conditions of service; see § 149.) The words which we have put in italics are important. It would seem to be contrary to the spirit of the White Paper to introduce, for instance, luncheon vouchers to a large staff. Moderate benefits in kind of a customary nature to senior executives

---

* Now Schedule 2 to the Act (see § 29).

would probably not be considered improper. A pension scheme to provide future benefits on retirement is a form of savings and it is therefore submitted that the introduction or improvement of such a scheme is unobjectionable. The difficulty, as already pointed out, is that the spirit of the freeze is one thing and the words of the threatened statutory control may be another. The Secretary of State may frame " descriptions of remuneration " under sections 28 and 29, which could be regarded as giving him power to extend the meaning of the word. On the other hand he defines the word for the purposes of sections which refer to " paying " remuneration and " rate " of remuneration, and in that context a widely extended meaning is difficult to envisage.

67. The application of the freeze to increased productivity is highlighted by the rejection by the Minister of Labour of the British Oxygen Company's new wages plan. This involved an increase in the hourly rates, but not it seems in the total earnings. It involved no increase in personal incomes, and therefore could have no inflationary effect. An increase in the output per man is something to be encouraged, but the White Paper of July 1966* (Cmnd. 3073) recognises this to a limited extent only in para. 18 (ii) which exempts from the standstill " piecework earnings, commissions on sales, any necessary increases in overtime worked, profit sharing schemes, etc.". There is no mention of increases in hourly rates due to increased productivity.

68. Restriction on increases of prices and charges.—The Secretary of State is empowered by order under section 26 (1) to apply that section to any prices for the sale of goods and to any charges for the performance of services, including any charges for the application of any process to goods. When an order has been so made, the prices or charges in question are not to be increased as from the date of the order unless the appropriate Minister gives his consent to an increase (section 26 (2)). The prohibition does not, however, apply in relation to prices paid on any sale by auction (section 26 (3)), the freezing of prices being hardly compatible with an auction sale and there is provision for excluding from the scope of the order prices and charges so far as practicable and appropriate for the purpose of ensuring that the section does nor impede the export trade (section 26 (6), and see § 118). Questions of discount are dealt with in section 26 (5), under which an order of the Secretary of State may provide for the manner in which account is to be taken of any discount and may be applied both to any price before discount is allowed and also to any price after it is allowed. Clearly, a reduction or removal of a discount habitually given can amount to an increase in price.

---

* Now Schedule 2 to the Act (see § 104).

69. Section 26 (4) seems to pile difficulty upon difficulty, and problem upon problem. It says that an order under subsection (1) of that section may frame a description of the prices or charges to which it refers *in any way* (our italics) and, in particular, in framing a description of prices of goods of a specified class, can make as many as four distinctions. The first of these is by reference to the undertakings or persons selling the goods, the second is by reference to the terms and conditions on which the goods are sold, the quantity sold or the undertakings or persons to whom they are sold, the third is by reference to the undertakings or persons by whom the goods have been produced or dealt with, or the locality in which they have been produced, while the fourth is to the effect that in making any of the distinctions above an order may distinguish undertakings or persons, by reference to the region or localities where they carry on business or the scale or turnover of their business or by reference to any other circumstances, and may include or exclude named undertakings or named persons. Comparable distinctions may be made in relation to charges for the performance of services.

70. The section, by subsection (7), imposes a maximum penalty on summary conviction of £100, and on indictment, of, if the offender is not a body corporate, £500 for any contravention of the prohibition in subsection (2) of price increases. See also, as to offences, § 175. A transaction is not, however, to be invalid in consequence of the provisions of the section, but a person paying an unlawful price or charge may recover the excess unless he is himself liable to be punished for having aided, abetted or procured the offence (subsection (1) of section 33). The section does not, at any rate, leave room for manoeuvre, though it has little else to commend its wording.

71. Restrictions on increases of prices and charges by reference to levels at 20th July 1966.—Under section 27, a Minister may give written notice to any person who was carrying on a business on 20th July 1966 (" D " day) which included the selling of goods or the performance of services to the effect that he, the Minister, is considering the giving of a direction under the section as respects the prices or charges for such services. This is an understandable, though stilted, piece of English, but then come the inevitable complications. Subsection (2) provides that a notice given as above is to give particulars of the proposed direction and is to specify a period, of not less than fourteen days from the service of the notice, within which that person may make written representations to the Minister. Here, at any rate, is some protection for the citizen on whom the Minister has served notice, though insufficient time is given to him to prepare the representations, which may be lengthy, contain many calculations and need to be closely argued.

72. Thereafter the Minister may, after the expiration of the period of notice and after considering any representations, serve a notice on

21

the person concerned directing that the section is to apply to such prices and charges of that person as may be specified in the direction (section 27 (3)). These prices or charges must then be reduced to a level not lower than that at which they stood on or before 20th July 1966 unless the Minister consents to, or the direction authorises, a lesser reduction (section 27 (4)).

73. A direction under the section may frame the descriptions of prices or charges in any way, and may contain particulars as to distinctions corresponding to those authorised by section 26 (4) of the Act (see § 69). There may also be the same provisions as in section 26 (5) as to discounts and again sales by auction are excluded (section 27 (5), (6)) (see §§ 68, 69).

74. A contravention of subsection (4) of the section is visited with the same penalties as a contravention of section 26 (2) (see § 70), and there is the same provision, made by section 33 (1), for recovery of an excess over a lawful price or charge. See also, as to offences, § 175.

75. **Restrictions on pay increases.**—The Secretary of State is empowered by section 28 to make orders providing that specified rates of remuneration are not to be increased beyond the rates obtaining before the coming into operation of the order unless the appropriate Minister gives his consent to an increase. On contravention of such an order an employer is liable on summary conviction to a maximum fine of £100, and on conviction on indictment, if not a body corporate, to a maximum fine of £500. See also, as to offences, § 175. The provisions of subsections (4)–(6) of section 16 as to attempting by strike or other action to induce an employer to implement a wage award or settlement are applied, as is also section 17, which defines a trade dispute (see § 165). The question of what is included in remuneration has been referred to § 66.

76. Although Part IV of the Act does not bind the Crown, an order may be made under this section or section 29 of this Act so as, without imposing any obligation on the Crown as an employer or otherwise, to apply to Crown employees, and subsections (4)–(6) of section 16 will accordingly apply to such employees (section 28 (5)).

77. An order under section 28 may frame the descriptions of remuneration in any way. In particular it may apply the section to employees in specified kinds of work, or in specified localities, or to employees working in specified undertakings or for specified employers.

78. Where an order applies the section to employees working in specified undertakings or for specified employers, it may make distinctions as regards those undertakings and persons by reference to the regions or localities where the undertakers or employers carry on

business, or in the number of persons working in the undertaking or for the employers, or by reference to any other different circumstances; and the order may be made so as to apply to named undertakings or persons (section 28 (7) (*b*)). An employer cannot recover from his employee any remuneration paid in excess of the permitted amount (section 33 (2)).

79. Scale rises in pay.—In para. 18 (iv) of Cmnd. 3073* it is stated that it is not intended that the freeze should be regarded as applying to " the normal arrangements for increasing pay either with age . . . or by means of regular increments of specified amounts within a pre-determined range or scale ". Already two schools of thought have placed their own interpretations upon the meaning of the words quoted. One school holds that these words mean that, if a job is in the £2000–£2500 range, increases within that range can be given without restriction but that range itself cannot be altered. The other school holds that, in the case of the job in question, increases of a discretionary nature would not be allowed even where a salary range exists for the job and a salary is undertaken at regular intervals. Which of the two schools is correct? There can be no certainty about this, though the second of the two interpretations has more support than the first. Where, however, the increments are at predetermined rates and of predetermined amounts the exemption obviously applies.

80. Restrictions on pay by reference to levels at 20th July 1966.— Under section 29 of the Act the Secretary of State is empowered to make an order providing that remuneration of the kind prescribed by the order is not, without Ministerial consent or as specified in the order, to be paid at a rate exceeding the rate paid for the same kind of work before 20th July 1966. The Secretary of State must give at least fourteen days' notice in the *Gazette* of his intention to make an order, within which time an employer, employers' organisation, trade union or trade union organisation may make representations. The same penalties as under section 28 are prescribed for contravention of the section and the pro-visions of section 28 (7) are applied (see § 75). The employer is not entitled to recover any remuneration paid over the permitted amount (section 33 (2)). See also, as to offences, § 175. The question of what constitutes " remuneration " has been referred to in § 66.

81. Existing contracts providing for pay increases.—As was pointed out in para. 19 of Cmnd. 3073* (see § 37), at least six million workers were expecting an increase in pay or a reduction in hours (or both) during the next twelve months as a result of long-term agreements or other types of settlement already made, and it would be inequitable to introduce a standstill on incomes and at the same time allow these

---

* Now Schedule 2 to the Act (see § 29).

existing commitments to go ahead unchecked. Hence the provisions of section 30 of the Act, which allow an employer to disregard pay increases due under existing contracts without incurring any liability in respect of breach of contract. Any increase withheld as a result of this section would not, of course, as was made clear by the Solicitor General in Committee, be recoverable later.

82. The section applies to any contract of employment made before the coming into force of Part IV of the Act under which a person who has worked for an employer since before that date is to receive remuneration for any period after that date at a higher rate than he was receiving before it. Provided that the employer gives one week's notice and pays or tenders remuneration for any period after the date, and while Part IV of the Act is in force, at the rate not less than the rate he paid immediately before, he is protected from any liability in respect of breach of contract in respect of failure to pay the higher rate of remuneration. It must, however, be emphasised that the employer's protection under the section arises only if Part IV has been brought into operation—unless and until this happens he must either pay the increase in accordance with the terms of the contract or arrive at a voluntary agreement with his employees not to pay it during the standstill period. The position of the employer during the voluntary freeze is hazardous, and at least one trade union has threatened to sue employers who disregard pay increases in existing contracts in accordance with the Government's request for voluntary pay restraint. It is an open question whether a collective bargain (as opposed to a contract of service) is legally enforceable, though the Contracts of Employment Act may be regarded as making the terms of the agreement part of the employee's contract. The threat however remains. A Conservative amendment at Report stage, which would have given protection during the voluntary freeze, was rejected, but the Attorney-General agreed that contracts remained valid, with the liabilities under them. He repeated that the advice of the Government to employers and workers was " Please, in this phase, come to terms remembering the public interest ".

83. Wage regulation orders.—Under section 11 (4) of the Wages Councils Act 1959, the Minister of Labour must, on receiving any wages regulation proposals, make an order giving effect to the proposals as from a date to be specified in the order, subject to a proviso whereby he may refer the proposals back for reconsideration by the wages council. There are at present some 57 wages councils governing the basic wages of approximately $3\frac{1}{2}$ million workers, and if no action were taken in respect of wage regulation orders and Part IV were to be brought into force, an anomaly would be created in that those covered by the orders would be exempt from its restrictions (see H. of C. Official Report S.C.B. col. 760).

84. The Minister of Labour is accordingly, by section 31 of the Act, absolved, so long as Part IV is in force, from the duty of making orders giving effect, under section 11 (4) of the Act of 1959, to wage regulation proposals, and the making of such an order and the date to be specified for its coming into operation are to be at his discretion, though the coming into operation of a proposal is not to be postponed beyond the period of twelve months mentioned in section 25 (1) of the Act (see § 63). The Minister may also vary, within the twelve month limit mentioned above, the date of operation of an order.

85. Agricultural workers.—Rates of wages and holidays for agricultural workers are fixed by the Agricultural Wages Board under the Agricultural Wages Act 1948 and the problem here is much the same as with wage regulation orders. Accordingly, the Minister of Agriculture, Fisheries and Food is empowered by section 32 of the Act to make orders deferring the coming into operation of orders of the Board to a date not later than the date fixed for the coming to an end of Part IV of the Act. An order of the Minister is not, however, to affect provisions which took effect before it was made.

86. Dividend restraint.—The Government has, as yet, no statutory powers over dividend payments. Nor is the Government presently seeking such powers; but Mr. George Brown, as Economic Affairs Minister, made it clear that if the dividend standstill is not observed, the Government will not hesitate to propose further action either in the form of separate legislation or of fiscal measures. The whole Prices and Incomes Act is, indeed, framed on the supposition that all sections of the community will support, without coercion or harsh persuasion, the Government's attempt to end inflation.

87. The freeze generally.—The broad intention of Government policy is to ensure that, in the months to the end of December, unwarranted increases in prices and incomes are altogether avoided. There will follow a six-month period of " severe restraint ". Industry and commerce, in fact the entire economy. are expected to make every effort to absorb increases in costs however they may arise. Relief from the chill of austerity will rarely be given: it will be given only where it can be shown that cost increases cannot possibly be absorbed. An increased cost of imported materials might be considered justification, or a rise in costs brought about by Government action such as increase of taxation or excise duties, or which is due to a seasonal pressure on supplies. Manufacturers whose products include a high proportion of bought-in components—assembly trades such as ship-building come in here—might also make out a good case for favoured treatment. Even so, any proposal by this category of industry to raise prices would, as was indicated in the " Prices and Income Standstill " White Paper*

---

* Now Schedule 2 to the Act (see § 29).

25

(Cmnd. 3073), be subjected to close search, in the light of the economic needs of the nation including the requirements of the export trade.

88. So far as wages and salaries are concerned a standstill on pay rises and the granting of shorter hours will remain in force until the close of the current calendar year. Then will follow six months of austerity. The exemptions described in § 36 apply. Agreements to pay increased wages or to shorten hours will be deferred by six months from the operative date if they were not effective before the basis date, 20th July. The British Oxygen Company and *Evening News* wages agreements were concluded, but not implemented, before 20th July, and were therefore deemed to come under the standstill. Even increases under schemes using the cost-of-living indices for the determination of wage rates will be invalid for the period between 20th July last and 30th June next. Nor will pay agreements concluded after 20th July become effective before 1st January 1967 at the earliest. All this is made clear by the White Paper of July 1966* (Cmnd. 3073).

---

6. REFERENCES TO THE PRICES AND INCOMES BOARD (PART I)

89. The Board and the " Freeze ".—In the provisions about the immediate prices and wages freeze, just described, there is no reference to the Prices and Incomes Board, and comment has been made upon the fact that the Board is not required to play any direct part in administering the immediate freeze. There is however nothing to prevent a Minister, who is asked to approve an increase of price or pay under the voluntary system or under sections 26–29, from referring the matter to the Board before making his decision. Indeed para. 37 of the White Paper of July 1966† (Cmnd. 3073) expresses the Government's intention to make the fullest use of the Board in this way.

90. The long-term functions of the Board.—It is noteworthy that although the urgent problem is the administration of the freeze whether on a voluntary or a compulsory basis, the most important part of the Act to operate immediately, and without any need for periodic renewal, is Part I, which establishes the National Board for Prices and Incomes, and governs references to the Board, and the continuous review of prices and incomes by the Board. This is permanent legislation, and is the foundation of the Government's long-term policy to control prices and wages.

91. Establishment of the Board.—The National Board for Prices and Incomes already existed on a non-statutory basis, having been appointed by Royal Warrant, and advised the Government within the White

---
* Now Schedule 2 to the Act (see § 29).
† Now Schedule 2 to the Act (see § 104).

Papers of April 1965 (Cmnd. 2639) and November 1965 (Cmnd. 2808), which latter is printed in the Appendix. It is now reconstituted on a statutory basis.

92. The main provisions as to the constitution of the Board are in section 1. It consists of not less than nine and not more than fifteen members appointed by the Secretary of State who may appoint persons to the Board either as full-time or part-time members. Of the full-time members, the Secretary of State appoints one to be Chairman of the Board and one or more to be deputy chairman or chairmen. Members of the Board will, of course, be renumerated.

93. Schedule 1, to which reference may be made for detail, contains full provisions for the tenure of office of members, chairman and deputy chairmen; disqualifies members from being Members of Parliament; and enables the Board to appoint officers and servants. It remains to be seen whether the Board can recruit sufficient staff of the right calibre, or whether the machinery will become clogged by an accumulation of work. Many Government Departments have yet fully to digest much of the legislation brought in by the present Government. Corporation tax and capital gains tax are examples of legislation whose hasty preparation has given rise to acute difficulties of administration. The Prices and Incomes Act seems likely, similarly, to become an administrative problem.

94. Provision is also made for the Board to determine its own procedure (subject to directions of the Secretary of State), and for the exercise of the Chairman's functions during absence or incapacity.

95. The Board enjoys, under subsection (6) of section 5, absolute privilege under the law of defamation in respect of its reports.

96. Expert panels.—A very valuable aid to the Board is provided by the two expert panels which the Secretary of State is to maintain under para. 11 of Schedule 1. One is of persons appearing to the Secretary of State to have special knowledge or experience of matters concerning employers and the other of persons having such knowledge or experience of employees.

97. Any matter before the Board must first, if the Chairman so directs, be considered by a group consisting of:—

(a) not less than three members of the Board nominated by the Chairman; and

(b) if he thinks fit, an equal number of persons nominated by him from each of the two expert panels.

The Board in reaching its decision must take into account the recommendations of the group, though it is not bound by them. The use of the panels ensures that both sides of a question will be thoroughly ventilated, and the success of these groups will largely determine the success of the Board as a whole. The Board will not, however, hand over authority or the power of decision to the experts; it is expressly stated in Schedule 1 that, in formulating a report, the Board will take into consideration, but will *not* be bound to accept, findings or recommendations of the examining group.

98. We are here considering the functioning of the Board. It is of course possible for the appropriate Minister himself to consult representatives of employers and employees direct.

99. Inquiries and disclosure of information.—Schedule 1 deals in paras. 13 and 14 with the obtaining of information by the Board. The Board or any group set up as above described are empowered to hold such inquiries as they find necessary or desirable for the discharge of their functions under the Act. The chairman of the Board or group can, at any such inquiry, direct that any person appearing as a witness be examined on oath, and may require any person to attend to give evidence on, or to produce documents which relate to, any matter in question at the inquiry. The chairman can also call upon any person engaged in trade or business, or any trade union or trade association, to supply the the Board or group with any needed returns, estimates or other information. These are far-reaching powers and are likely to be used, but no person can be compelled to give evidence or to produce documents which he could not be compelled to give or produce before the High Court.

100. The interests of those who are thus required to give information to the Board are protected by para. 16, which limits the persons to whom such information may be disclosed, without the consent of the person giving the information. It is also relevant that in subsection (5) of section 5 the Board in framing its reports is required, as far as practicable, to exclude matter referring to the private affairs of anyone who might be prejudiced by its publication.

101. References to the Board.—Having discussed the establishment and procedure of the Prices and Incomes Board we will examine how matters get on to its agenda. The first, and most obvious, method is when the Secretary of State (or the Secretary and another Minister jointly) refer a matter specifically to the Board under section 2 of the Act. A reference may be withdrawn or varied by a further reference. All references must be published in the Gazette. They may apply to particular localities or to named undertakings or persons. The Board must examine the matter and make a report, which is dealt with as described in § 106.

102. Matters which may be referred to the Board.—The Act sets out, in section 2, two particular groups of matters which may be referred, and with which indeed the whole system is mainly concerned, namely questions:

" (*a*) relating to a proposal to increase prices for the sale of goods or any charges for the performance of services, including charges for the application of any process to goods, or

(*b*) relating to any pay claims or other claims relating to terms and conditions of employment, or any awards and settlements relating to terms and conditions of employment."

But although these matters are particularised in section 2 (and they are matters with which the " early-warning " and standstill provisions in Part II of the Act are concerned, see §§ 107–166), yet the general provisions of the section are much wider in scope, since there may be referred to the Board:

" any question relating to wages, salaries or other forms of incomes, or to prices, charges or other sums payable under transactions of any description relating to any forms of property or rights or to services of any description or to returns on capital invested in any form of property, including company dividends."

This covers practically every form of commercial transaction which can be imagined, and certainly covers building society mortgages. When we consider the " early-warning " system and the immediate freeze we shall see that they may well be much narrower in scope.

103. Continuous review by the Board.—The arrangements under section 3 for continuous review by the Board (as opposed to specific reference to the Board) do not immediately operate. First the Secretary of State must make an order applying the section to particular groups of incomes or prices or charges or other matters, which he is empowered to refer to the Board under section 2 (see § 102). The scope of the two sections is therefore basically equally wide. Having applied the section by order, he then instructs the Board to keep under review all or any of the matters in the order. The Board then reports, whenever it thinks fit, or when the Secretary of State requires it to. The reports are dealt with as described in § 106.

Orders and instructions may apply to particular localities or to named undertakings or persons. Orders are issued by the Stationery Office as Statutory Instruments, and instructions are published in the *Gazette*. An instruction may be varied or withdrawn by a further instruction, but clearly the intention is that they should normally continue, so as to provide a " continuous review ".

104. Principles to be applied by the Board.—Section 4 requires the Board, in exercising its functions, to have regard to the considerations set out in Schedule 2. These were originally a reproduction of Part I of the White Paper " Prices and Incomes Policy " presented to Parliament in April 1965 (Cmnd. 2639) (see §§ 17–23). The Secretary of State has, however, by virtue of powers contained in section 4 (2) (see § 105) made on August 12th the Prices and Incomes (General Considerations) Order, 1966 (S.I. 1966 No. 1021), which substitutes the provisions of the White Paper of July 1966, " Prices and Incomes Standstill " (Cmnd. 3073) (see §§ 29–45), and the Schedule as so substituted now governs the operations of the Board. It is printed at p. [*58*] of this book.

105. The Secretary of State may make orders varying the considerations set out in Schedule 2. Such orders are published as Statutory Instruments. After February 11th, 1967, such orders may only be made after consulting with interested organisations. The first such order is mentioned in § 104.

106. The Reports of the Board.—The Reports of the Board must under section 5 be laid before Parliament and must be published in the manner considered appropriate by the Minister or Ministers concerned. Moreover the date of publication must be notified in the *Gazette.* These requirements should ensure that the decisions of the Board receive a sufficient publicity. Other requirements make sure that the " interests of national security " are protected. Subsection (2) of section 5 says that, if it appears to the Minister or Ministers concerned that the publication of any matter in the report would be against such interests, the Ministers in question can exclude that matter from the copies of the report laid before Parliament and later published. In the same way the rights of the individual are looked after; subsection (5) of section 5 states that, in framing a report the Board must have in mind the need for excluding, so far as is possible, any matter relating to the private affairs of any person the publication of which could prejudicially affect that person's interests. A time limit of three months after the reference or request for report is set in the Act for the publication of Board Reports. A strict adherence to these limits may, at times, prove difficult. It is presumably for this reason that the Minister or Ministers concerned with a particular report may extend the time by direction published in the *Gazette.* The date of publication is however vital to the working of the Government's " early-warning " and standstill system, should that receive the force of law (see § 108), since the standstill ceases after three months.

---

7. THE " EARLY-WARNING " SYSTEM (PART II)

107. We have considered two of the three prongs of the Government attack on inflation—the immediate price and wage freeze (whether voluntary, or compulsory under Part IV of the Act) and the long-term system of reports by the Prices and Wages Board (which is already in full operation). The third prong was described in the White Paper dated November 1965 headed " Prices and Incomes Policy: an ' Early-Warning ' System " (Cmnd. 2808), which is printed in the Appendix to this book. Part II of the Prices and Incomes Act 1966 gives statutory effect to this system, whereby notification can be required of increases in prices and charges, of increases in dividends, and of increases in wages and salaries. In relation to prices and charges, and to wages and salaries (but not to dividends) a standstill is imposed while the Minister decides whether to refer the matter to the Board, and (if he does so) while the Board prepares its report. This part of this Act is not at present in force. In any case it would be subject to the immediate price and wages freeze, whether voluntary or statutory.

108. Bringing Part II into operation. The process of bringing Part II into operation falls into two main stages—first an Order in Council bringing provisions into force, and second (in relation to some of the provisions) an order of the Secretary of State applying a particular section to particular persons or transactions. We are here concerned with the first of these stages, but it should be noticed that an order at the second stage can be made before, though it cannot come into operation before, the Order in Council at the first stage.

109. Before an Order in Council is drafted the Secretary of State must consult (though he need not take the advice of) such organisations or bodies as he thinks fit. They must appear to him substantially to represent the interests of those particularly concerned with the Order. The point to make here, and it is of some importance, is that very wide power of decision is left with the Secretary of State. " As he thinks fit " could mean no consultation at all.

110. After the Order in Council is drafted it must be laid before Parliament in draft, and approved by both Houses of Parliament, before it can be made. This is the principal safeguard against the abuse of his powers by the Secretary of State.

111. The Order in Council may bring into operation either the provisions as to prices and dividends, or the provisions as to wages, or all three. It cannot however deal separately with prices and dividends. The provisions in question are brought into force for twelve months at a time (though their operation may be put an end to at any time by a further order). If one group of provisions is already in force the other group may be brought in for the residue of the twelve months, or independently for a full twelve months.

Prices and Charges

112. Prices and charges generally.—Section 7 deals with notices of intention to increase prices, and provides for a standstill while the appropriate Minister decides whether to refer the matter to the Board and, if he so decides, pending the report of the Board. This section applies to such prices and charges as may be indicated in an order of the Secretary of State. These provisions are more fully described in §§ 113–116. Section 8 imposes a corresponding standstill where the Secretary of State refers a matter to the Board without having received a notification of increase (see § 117). The supplementary provisions of sections 9 to 11 are described in §§ 118–126.

113. Application of section 7 to particular goods or services.—The Secretary of State may by order apply section 7 to " any prices for the sale of goods and to any charges for the performance of services, including charges for the application of any process to goods ". It should be noted that these words are considerably narrower than those of section 2 (1), which lists all the matters which the Secretary of State may refer to the Prices and Incomes Board (see § 102). In specifying the goods and services to which an order applies the order may distinguish by reference to the seller, the terms of sale, the quantity sold, the buyer, the producer, the locality of manufacture, the place where any of the foregoing carry on business, and the scale of their business, and may refer to named undertakings or persons. It is clear that the net may be cast wide, or may be highly selective. The order may take account of discounts, and it may apply to a price before discount and also after discount. This would cover, for instance, an attempt to increase revenue by varying discounts.

114. Notification of increases.—Notice of a proposed increase in prices or charges in respect of goods or services, to which section 7 has been applied as described in the previous paragraph, must be given to the appropriate Minister under subsection (2) of section 7. It is an offence to increase prices or charges by any amount unless notice of intention to increase them " by at least that amount " has been given. A notice therefore covers an increase of a smaller amount than that named in it; in other words a fresh notice need not be given if it is subsequently decided to reduce the increase. It is arguable that the wording would also cover making a notified increase in two instalments. When the notice has been given the standstill described in the next paragraph applies.

115. Temporary standstill.—When the notice has been given one of four things may happen.

(1) The appropriate Minister may take no action; in that case the price may not be increased until the expiration of thirty days beginning with the day on which the notice of intention was given.

(2) The appropriate Minister may give notice that he does not propose to refer the matter to the Prices and Incomes Board;

in that case the price may be increased on receipt of the notice.

(3) The appropriate Minister may refer the matter to the Board by a reference published in the *Gazette* within the thirty days period named in (1) above; in that case the price may not be increased until publication of the Board's report (which may under subsection (2) of section 19 be an interim report).

(4) The appropriate Minister may give his written consent to the increase before publication of the report (such consent to be notified in the *Gazette*).

These provisions are contained in subsection (3) of section 7.

116. If the Board's report is not published within three months of the publication of the reference to the Board in the *Gazette*, it is provided that the standstill shall cease at the end of the three month period. It is clearly desirable that the report should be in the hands of the Minister well before the expiry of the three month period, in order that any discussions of the Board's recommendations can take place during the standstill period.

117. Standstill for prices or charges referred to the Board.—The provisions just described apply where notification is required in respect of particular goods or services. The power of the Secretary of State under section 2 (see § 102) to refer matters to the Board is not limited but he may make a reference in respect of any goods or services. Where (without receiving any notification) he makes a reference in respect of " prices for the sale of goods or charges for the performance of services, including charges for the application of any process ", the Secretary of State may in the same issue of the *Gazette* direct that section 8 shall apply. Subsection (2) of section 8 provides that prices and charges to which the section applies may not be increased until publication of the Board's report, or until the reference is revoked in whole, or is revoked as to the relevant part. The Board's report may be an interim one, and if it is not published within three months the standstill ends at the expiry of three months (section 19). It is to be observed that this standstill arrangement only applies to goods and services within the exact wording of section 8, and does not apply to all the matters which can be referred to the Board under section 2 (see § 102).

118. Export trade.—It is provided by subsection (1) of section 9 that the standstill provisions outlined above, that is to say an order of the Secretary of State under section 7 and a direction of the Secretary of State under section 8 " shall contain such provisions for excluding prices and charges as appear to the Minister or Ministers making the order or giving the direction practicable and appropriate for the purpose of ensuring that those sections do not impede export trade (that is to say, the provision of goods and services for persons not resident in the United Kingdom) ''. As so much of the Government's policy of restraint on prices and incomes inevitably adds to the difficulties of export traders either directly or indirectly, it is good to see this official recognition of their importance. Nevertheless it is to be noted that, in spite of the importance of the export trade as an earner of foreign exchange and a contributor on the credit side of the balance of trade, nothing is said of the need to *encourage* export trade.

119. U.K. companies and firms with large overseas subsidiaries or affiliates have their own special problems. What, for instance, happens to U.K. concerns which operate joint ventures in foreign parts and thereby attract a currency flow to this country? There are often, in such cases, mutual pricing arrangements of all-round benefit and helpful to sterling. Must the U.K. concerns that come into this category of overseas trading hold their prices and thereby prevent their overseas partners from making price increases with detriment to U.K. receipts of currency from abroad?

120. Prices governed by other enactments.—Schedule 3 to the Act, to which reference should be made, excludes, wholly or in part, from the operation of the notification and standstill arrangements the prices and charges governed by the enactments listed in paragraph 2 of that Schedule. The price-regulating bodies in question are however required by section 23 to have regard to the considerations referred to in section 4 and Schedule 2 (see §§ 104, 29–45).

121. Auction sales. The notification and standstill arrangements do not apply to auction sales (subsection (4) of section 9).

122. Validity of transactions.—A transaction is not invalid because it involves a forbidden price or charge, but the payer can recover the excess, unless he is himself liable to punishment for aiding and abetting the offence (subsection (4) of section 9).

123. Where a transaction is carried out under an enforceable contract concluded before the order under section 7 or the direction under section 8, the notification and standstill provisions do not apply.

124. Comparison of prices and charges.—In ascertaining whether a price or charge has been increased the rules of section 10 have to be observed. It is to be observed that when there are no goods (or services) of the same description with which a comparison can be made, the most similar goods or services of the same person must be used for comparison, with a fair adjustment to take account of the differences.

125. Enforcement.—We now come to the matter of enforcement of the provisions of the Act so far as they concern prices and charges. Section 11 lays down that it will be an offence for any person in the course of business to sell, agree to sell or offer to sell any goods or to perform, agree to perform or offer to perform any service if the price for the goods or services represents an increase forbidden under the Act. It is a defence to show that a similar price was being asked before the notification and standstill arrangements began to operate. Fines can be imposed for an offence under this as under other sections of the Act but, in many cases, the punishment inflicted seems hardly to fit the crime. Fines of not exceeding one hundred pounds on summary conviction and not exceeding five hundred pounds on conviction on indictment if the offender is not a body corporate are not punitive. On the other hand there is no limit to the fine which may be imposed on indictment on a body corporate, which of course includes every company.

126. An agreement, or offer, or notice of price or charge may be made when the increase is forbidden if its terms preclude the sale or performance of services while the increase is forbidden (subsection (3) of section 11).

Company Distributions

127. Outline of provisions.—Section 12 requires companies to notify the appropriate Minister of increases in distributions within one week of the relevant decision. There is no standstill provision, and the notification is intended to assist the Secretary of State and the Ministers to decide whether to refer any matter to the Prices and Incomes Board.

128. The section does not operate until applied by order of the Secretary of State, which will be published as a Statutory Instrument. The order may apply by reference to the nature or scale or locality of a business, and may include or exclude named companies.

129. Not many companies would wish to step up dividend payments in the coming months: the profits will not be there to justify this and the outlook is too uncertain. But the Government has to control dividend distributions, just as it has to control receipts from all other sources, in an Act which erects a ceiling over prices and incomes. No one part of the community can be left outside the discipline of a regulated economy.

130. It has been suggested that to apply the " early-warning " system to dividends looked absurd, since such decisions had, by the rules of the Stock Exchange, to be announced at once. This however only applies to quoted companies, whereas the " early-warning " system can be applied to all companies, including private companies.

131. Orders of the Secretary of State.—Subsection (1) of Section 12 reads thus:

" With a view to obtaining information regarding increases in company distributions which may assist the Secretary of State and other Ministers to determine whether any question concerning any company or companies should be referred to the Board under section 2 of this Act, or whether any instruction or requirement should be given to or imposed on the Board under section 3 of this Act, the Secretary of State may, by order apply this section to any companies."

He is thus given a very broad authority.

132. Equally far-reaching is the authority given the Secretary of State under subsection (2) of section 12. This says that an order under subsection (1) may frame a description of companies to which this section applies *in any way* and particularly can make distinctions by reference to the nature or scale of the trade or business carried on by any company, or the locality in which it is carried on, and can include or exclude named companies. This *carte blanche* arrangement seems to give the Minister too much freedom of action, but present circumstances are abnormal and may satisfy a temporary departure from the traditional relationship between Government and industry in a democratic economy. Besides, it has been the evident intention of the Government so to frame the Prices and Incomes Act that, as far as possible, it can always extend a helping hand to the needy and the deserving—as for instance the areas of exceptionally high unemployment, the small man fighting for a place in the sun and the export trader.

133. Basis year.—Any increase in distributions made by a company to which section 12 applies must be ascertained by reference to an earlier financial year, described as the " basis financial year ". The rules for determining the " basis financial year " will be contained in an order of the Secretary of State, published as a Statutory Instrument.

134. The rules may designate different basis financial years for successive financial years of the same company, may make different provisions for different descriptions of companies to which section 12 applies and may fix a basis financial year which falls wholly or partly before the time when section 12 begins to apply to the company. Once again the Act gives the Government far-ranging powers which will and must be used rather to further Government policies than to solace the investor.

135. It cannot be said that the account given by Mr. George Brown in the Standing Committee on the Bill did much to clear the air. He said:

" The criterion of a base year will have to be prescribed differently for different companies or different groups. These things fluctuate greatly. If one simply said that a certain year was the base year, a very unfair comparison could be obtained in another year. We have written it in such a form that we shall be able to prescribe

the base year in the circumstances either of a company or the group of companies being dealt with. We do not see how else it can be done if it is desired to secure a fair comparison to show a true picture where increases in distribution are really taking place."
This is confusion worse confounded. Can it be that companies will be allotted the basis year most favourable to them?

136. Notification of increase.—Subsection (4) of section 12 orders that, if the amount of the distributions to be made by a company to which this section applies for any financial year beginning at a time when this section applies to the company, with any adjustment required by subsection (7) (see § 141), will exceed the amount of distributions made by the company for its basis financial year, the company must, not more than seven days after the date when the relevant distribution (see § 144) was made, notify the appropriate Minister and let him have full particulars of the distributions made or to be made in the respective financial years. The company has also to specify the amount of the excess.

137. If a decision is changed, or a further decision is made, or an assumption proves wrong, the notification must be corrected under subsection (5) within seven days.

138. A failure to comply with subsection (4) or (5) renders a company liable to a fine not exceeding £50 on summary conviction.

139. Meaning of distribution.—" Distribution " is defined by subsection (10) of section 12 as having the same meaning as in Part I of Schedule 11 to the Finance Act 1965, which is reproduced in the notes in section 12 in this book. (See also *Simon's Income Tax*, Vol. 2A, §§ 576–581; *Beattie's Corporation Tax*, pp. 80–83.) It is to be noted in this connection that the Act only requires notification of dividend increases, and that any dividend limitation is at present voluntary. In asking for the voluntary freeze in the White Paper of July 1966 (Cmnd. 3073) an exception is made for close companies who are, it appears, permitted to make distributions up to the proportions required by the corporation tax laws (see para. 31 of Cmnd. 3073).

140. " Scrip " or bonus issues are not normally a distribution within the meaning of the Finance Act 1965 (see *Simon's Income Tax*, Vol. 2A, §§ 578–580; *Beattie's Corporation Tax*, p. 82).

141. Adjustment of capital.—Subsection (7), referred to in § 136, provides that the amount of the distributions made by a company for any financial year shall, for the purpose of determining whether there is a dividend increase, be adjusted in proportion to the amount by which the issued share capital of the company at the beginning of the financial year exceeds, or is less than, the issued share capital at the beginning of the basis financial year. Allowance is thus made for any issue of capital by the company for cash, in exchange for shares in another concern or for a purchase of the assets of another concern. The " amount or value of any consideration actually received " is to be added to the share capital. An issue of bonus shares would not, it appears come into the calculation. Such an issue is merely a transfer from reserves to the capital account—a move from one entry in the balance sheet to another. A diminution of the amount of the issued share capital over a financial year could result from a repayment of capital made possible by a sale of assets or transfer of money. A reduction of capital by way of a writing down when values have been permanently lost would not, apparently, come into this category. The effect of subsection (7) in connection with rights issues has been questioned. Is it the nominal value or the consideration for the new shares (that is the nominal value plus the premium) which has to be added? In other words if one new £1 share is issued, for the price of £2, for each existing £1 share held, is the issued share capital doubled or trebled?

142. After the making of all required adjustments the amount of company's share capital at the commencement of the basis financial year is defined in the final paragraph of subsection (7) as being made up of what is then the amount of the paid-up capital and of any share premium account or other comparable account however labelled. This definition could give rise to much argument, though the bringing into the calculation of a share premium or comparable account is to be commended. Such balances are part of shareholders' capital since they largely represent monies subscribed by shareholders on the occasion of issues made at a premium over par or nominal value. Free reserves are, of course, also shareholders' property, but it would be contrary to all practice to consider an increase of free reserves as an increase in the issued share capital.

143. One other adjustment also is required by subsection (7), namely where the length of the financial year differs. In giving notice of increase any reasonable assumption may be made as to the length of the current financial year, but if that is other than twelve months the notice must state that the assumption has been made and state the length assumed (subsection (9)).

144. The relevant decision.—Notification is required within seven days of the relevant decision. These words mean, according to subsection (8) (*a*), where only one distribution is made by a company in the financial year, the decision to make that distribution. In any other cases they mean (see subsection (8) (*b*)) any decision the implementation of which will bring the distributions made or to be made by a company for the financial year, with any adjustments that subsection (7) may call for, into excess of the amount of the distributions made by the company for its basis financial year.

145. In deciding under subsection (8) (*b*) whether the distribution is in excess, and whether in consequence notice under subsection (4) is needed it must be assumed that any preference dividend falling due after the taking of the decision in question and any interest on securities of the company falling due after that time will, in fact, be paid.

146. " Decision " means the effective decision, which may be a declaration of dividend by the company in general meeting, or a decision of the directors, or any other decision, except that where the directors decide to recommend a dividend to be declared by the company in general meeting that decision and not the declaration of the dividend in general meeting will be the decision for the purpose of section 12. The point is one that company secretaries must watch very carefully.

147. General comments.—Section 12 of the Prices and Incomes Act has given the financial columns an exceptional opportunity—which has been seized—of ferreting out anomalies. There has been specially mentioned in the Investors Chronicle the case of Jaguar shareholders who get an effective increase of dividend when Jaguar is taken over by the British Motor Corporation. How do they stand under the Act? And what of the shareholders in companies that have paid no dividends for years but, because of an improved earning position, are now able to make a distribution. Is their special position not to be recognised? Are any exceptions to be made for hard cases?

148. The date of July 20, however, only applies to the voluntary dividend freeze for which the Government has asked as from that date, and it remains to be seen whether the particular example cited will be relevant by the time the " early-warning " system under section 12 is introduced. When it is introduced the comparison is between one financial year and another, and July 20 is not the dividing line.

Pay and Terms of Employment

149. There are two main limbs to the " early warning " system relating to terms and conditions of employment. Both have to be brought into operation by order of the Secretary of State, which is published as a Statutory Instrument. The first, under section 13, requires notice to be given of pay and other claims. No standstill provision arises. The second, under section 14, requires notice to be given of awards and settlements. This results in a standstill while the appropriate Minister decides whether to refer the matter to the Board, and (if he does so) while the Board prepares its report. A standstill may also be imposed when a reference is made to the Board apart from a notification. It should be noted that the awards and settlements, to which these notification and standstill provisions apply, relate not only to pay, but also to other terms and conditions of service. The provisions could therefore relate to " fringe " benefits and benefits in kind, in so far as these are within awards and settlements. However the orders to be made under the Act will make clear the exact scope of the matters to be notified. (Compare § 66 as to " fringe benefits " during the freeze period.)

150. Notices of pay claims and other claims.—The Secretary of State may by order (published as a Statutory Instrument) apply section 13 to any pay claims or other claims relating to terms and conditions of employment made on behalf of employees. The order may by virtue of subsection (6) specify the claims to which the section is to apply in any way, including specified kinds of work, specified localities, or specified employees. Different classes of employee of the same employer may be distinguished, and the number of employees may be taken into account. Pay claims and other claims may also be distinguished.

151. Notice of any claim to which the section applies must be given to the appropriate Minister within seven days of its being presented to the employer or employers' organisation (subsection (2)). It may be given either by the claimant or trade union, or by the employer or employers' organisation (subsection (3)). Both are equally responsible for ensuring that the notice is given, and either party is liable on failure to notify to a fine not exceeding £50 on summary conviction (subsection (4)). A trade union accepts responsibility by notice to the Secretary of State, which will be approved by him by notice in the *Gazette* if he is satisfied that the persons for whom the trade union is acting agree to its so doing (subsection (5)).

152. This section does not apply to claims made before there is an order in force embracing that claim (subsection (7)).

153. The section makes no provisions for any action by the appropriate Minister, and the notification is for information purposes.

154. Notices of awards and settlements.—The Secretary of State may by order (published as a Statutory Instrument) apply section 14 to any awards or settlements relating to terms or conditions of service. The provisions of subsection (6) of section 13 (see § 150) are applied by subsection (7) to the framing of the order.

155. Notice of an award or settlement must be made within seven days to the appropriate Minister, with particulars thereof, and the penalty for failure is a fine not exceeding £50 on summary conviction (subsection (2)). A notice may be given by one employer on behalf of others or by an employers' organisation. It may also be given by a trade union or other person representing the employees, in which case the employer is absolved from his responsibility (subsection (3)). The prime responsibility is however on the employer, and (unlike under section 13, see § 151) the employees or trade union cannot be fined for failure to give notice.

156. On receipt of a notice the appropriate Minister must notify the receipt in the *Gazette* (subsection (4)).

157. No award or settlement may be implemented unless notice has been given (subsection (5)), nor may it be implemented during a standstill period (subsection (6)), as described in §§ 159, 160.

158. The section does not apply to an award or settlement made before there is an order in force embracing that kind of award or settlement (subsection (8)).

159. Temporary standstill.—When notice has been given of the award or settlement one of four things may happen:

(1) The appropriate Minister may take no action; in that case the award or settlement may not be implemented until after the expiration of thirty days beginning with the date on which notice was given.

(2) The appropriate Minister may publish a notice in the *Gazette* that it has been decided not to refer the matter to the Board; in that case the award may be given effect to forthwith.

(3) The appropriate Minister may refer the matter to the Board by a reference published in the *Gazette* within the thirty day period named in (1) above; in that case the award or settlement may not be given effect to until the publication of the Board's report (which may under subsection (2) of section 19 be an interim report).

(4) The appropriate Minister may give his written consent to the implementation of the award or settlement before the publication of the report (such consent to be notified in the *Gazette*).

These provisions are contained in subsection (6) of section 14.

160. If the Board's report is not published within three months of the publication of the reference to the Board in the *Gazette*, it is provided that the standstill shall cease at the end of the three month period (subsection (1) of section 19). It is clearly desirable that the report should be in the hands of the Minister well before the expiry of the three month period, in order that any discussions of the Board's recommendations can take place during the standstill period.

41

161. Standstill for awards and settlements referred to the Board.— Where the Secretary of State refers to the Board an award or settlement of which he has received no notification, including presumably one to which section 14 (see § 154) does not apply, he may by notice in the same issue of the *Gazette* direct that section 15 shall apply. In that event the award or settlement may not be implemented until publication of the Board's report, or until the reference is revoked in whole, or is revoked as to the relevant part (subsection (2) of section 15). The Board's report may be an interim one, and if it is not published within three months the standstill ends at the expiry of three months (subsection (1) of section 19).

162. Section 15 does not apply to an employer who implements the award or settlement before the direction is published in the *Gazette* (subsection (3) of section 15).

163. Enforcement generally.—An employer who implements an award or settlement while it is forbidden, is liable to a fine not exceeding £100 on summary conviction, or on indictment to a fine of an unlimited amount on a body corporate (including any company), or not exceeding £500 in the case of other persons (subsections (1) and (3) of section 16).

164. It is however not unlawful for an employer to pay remuneration in respect of earlier employment at a time when the implementation of the award or settlement is not forbidden (subsection (2)). In other words an award may be back dated after the standstill period.

165. Trade disputes.—Strike action to influence an employer to implement an award or settlement when it is forbidden makes the persons instigating, threatening or taking part in the strike liable to the same penalties as the employer would be liable to if he implemented the award (subsection (4) of section 16). This does not give rise to any further criminal or tortious liability (or any civil liability in Scotland) (subsections (5) and (6)). Any dispute arising out of the restrictions imposed by Part II of the Act is included in the expression " trade dispute " as defined by section 5 (3) of the Trade Disputes Act 1906 (see section 17).

166. Crown employment.—Employment under the Crown (including national health service employment) does not normally come within Part II, which does not bind the Crown. But a standstill may be imposed (though not so as to impose any liability on the Crown) under s. 15 (see § 161), and the provisions as to trade disputes apply to Crown employees (see § 165).

---

8. MISCELLANEOUS PROVISIONS

167. Definitions.—Subsection (1) of section 34 states the meaning for the purpose of this Act of the expressions " Minister ", " appropriate

Minister " (see §§ 177, 178), " employee ", " trade association " and " trade union ".   What is more important, it extends, in some cases quite remarkably, the meaning of certain expressions.

168. " Awards and settlements " in relation to terms or conditions of employment, includes any agreement to which an employer or an employers' organisation is a party, whether or not enforceable in law, and whether or not concluded under recognised arrangements.

169. The expression " in the course of business " includes " in the course of any trade, profession or vocation."

170. " Goods " includes " ships and aircraft, minerals, substances and animals (including fish)".

171. " Price " includes a charge of any description. This is important since, although the Act usually refers to " prices and charges " it does not always do so.

172. " Public notice " is extended to cover a notice given by a member of a trade association to other members.

173. The Gazette.   References are made throughout the Act, and throughout this narrative to " the *Gazette* " rather than to the " *London Gazette* ", since publication may be in either the *London Gazette*, or the *Edinburgh Gazette* or the *Belfast Gazette*, or in two or three of these, according to the local application of the matters to be published.   Where the publication date is different, the matter is treated as published on the earliest date.

174. Offences and penalties.—The penalties for offences under the Act have already been mentioned under the appropriate provisions. No proceedings may be taken without the consent of the Attorney-General (in England and Wales) and the Attorney-General for Northern Ireland (in Northern Ireland).

Where an offence is committed by a trade union, trade union organisation or employers' organisation which is an unincorporated body, the proceedings must be brought in the name of that body, and fines paid out of the funds of the body. Various procedural matters are to be applied as if the body were a corporation. There seems, however, to be no provision whereby the fine can exceed £500, whereas for bodies corporate there is no limit to the fine on indictment.

175. Where an offence committed by a body corporate is proved to have been committed with the consent or connivance of, or to be attributable to any neglect on the part of, any director, manager, secretary or other similar officer of the body corporate, he as well as the body corporate shall be deemed guilty of that offence and will be liable to be proceeded against and to be punished accordingly. It is, however, right that where directors and officers of a company have been found guilty of neglect or worse in the performance of their duties, they should be suitably punished. That these duties are being made unbearably heavy by the filling in of innumerable forms or the supply of masses of information for the benefit of Government departments is no more an excuse for breaking the law than is ignorance of the law.

176. All the above provisions are contained in section 22 in relation to offences under Part II (" early-warning " and standstill), and are applied under Part IV (the " freeze " provisions) by subsection (6) of section 25.

177. Notices.—The Secretary of State may prescribe the method and form of giving notices, and in particular may define the " appropriate Minister " for the purposes of any notice. This provision is contained in section 21 in relation Part II (" early-warning " and standstill), and is applied to Part IV (the " freeze " provisions) by subsection (6) of section 25.

178. The question of " appropriate Minister " has given rise to much anxiety. Some guidance is given by Part A of the Appendix to the White Paper of November 1965 (Cmnd. 2808), but this list is provisional only, and in the meantime applications for permission to increase prices or wages will be needed over a much wider field during the " freeze " and the period of severe restraint—whether voluntary or compulsory.

---

9. SPECIAL APPLICATIONS OF THE ACT

179. Conditional sale and hire-purchase agreements.—The Act applies, by virtue of subsection (3) of section 34, in relation to

(*a*) a conditional sale agreement, and

(*b*) a hire-purchase agreement,

as if the agreement were a sale of goods to which the agreement relates for an amount equal to the total purchase price with a fair reduction where the consideration for receipt of that price includes the installation, maintenance or repair of the goods or performance of other services apart from the giving of credit. Subsection (3) is to be construed in accordance with the Hire-Purchase Act 1965, and (in relation to Scotland) the Hire-Purchase (Scotland) Act 1965.

180. Directors and executives.—Directors and executives, and indeed other workers not subject to wage awards and settlements, are not covered by Part II (the " early warning " and temporary standstill provisions) but they are within the immediate freeze provisions of Part IV (§§ 63–88). Their position is clarified by para. 28 of the White Paper of July 1966 (Cmnd. 3073)*. It points out that many individual salaries and

---

* Now Schedule 2 to the Act (see § 104).

other forms of remuneration, including that of company directors and executives, are fixed outside the normal process of collective bargaining. It is rightly intended that the principles of standstill and restraint shall apply to these as to other forms of income. More than that, the White Paper reminds directors and others that a Companies Bill, to be introduced in Parliament during the present session, will incorporate certain statutory requirements relating to the disclosure by companies of emoluments of directors and senior executives. Some directors have been incensed by this reminder and see in it a veiled threat. The question of " fringe-benefits " during the freeze period is discussed in § 66.

181. Professional men.—Professional men may become subject to the provisions of sections 7 to 11 (the " early warning " and temporary standstill) in respect of charges for services (see §§ 112–126). They can also come within section 26 and 27 (the statutory freeze) (see §§ 68–74), since those sections refer to charges for services. Meanwhile during the immediate voluntary freeze the White Paper of July 1966* (Cmnd. 3073) reminds professional men, in para. 29, that the scales of charges and fees for self-employed persons, including all forms of professional fees, are expected to be under similar restraint for the twelve months as other forms of employment income.

182. Public services and nationalised industries.—Paras. 32 to 36 of the White Paper of July 1966* remind Government Departments, public services and nationalised industries of their duties. The Government means to enforce standstill discipline upon all prices, charges and fees of Government Departments, whilst employers and workers in the public services and publicly-owned undertakings will be considered to have the same obligations as the rest of the community to act at all times with the national interest predominantly in mind.

183. The nationalised industries cannot contract out of standstill agreements. They will, in relation to prices and incomes, be subject to the same restraint as the private sector of the economy. They will also be bound by the general provision set out in the Prices and Incomes Act. Statutorily established price-fixing bodies such as the Traffic Commissioners and the Transport Tribunal are similarly reminded of their crisis duties.

184. Although the Crown is not bound by Parts II and IV of the Act, the standstill provisions of section 15 (see § 161) and the freeze provisions of sections 28 and 29 (see §§ 75–80) apply to those employed by the Crown (including those in the National Health Service) (see section 18 and subsection (5) of section 28).

185. Rents and rates.—The Government's policy in regard to rents and rates during the voluntary periods of freeze and severe restraint

---

* Now Schedule 2 to the Act (see § 104).

is set out in paras. 11 to 14 of the White Paper of July 1966* (Cmnd. 3073). The first deals with private housing rents, the second with council house rents, the third with business premises, and the fourth with rates.

186. " The level of rents charged by landlords for virtually the whole of the private housing sector is already ", the White Paper* points out, " determined within the statutory framework of the Rent Acts, but the Government will keep under the closest scrutiny the movements of rents of private housing." Local authority rents are on a non-profit-making and subsidised basis. From this it follows that, if higher costs are not met from rents they must be recouped from rates. But these, too, are a charge on tenants. The Government has made known that, in the standstill period until the close of 1966, it expects local authorities to take all steps possible to prevent or postpone rent increases, including increases already announced. Special help should be given to the poorer tenants through rent rebate schemes whilst other public authorities, such as those in charge of the new towns, are expected to conform to the rules of conduct drawn up for the local authorities. The reaction of local authorities to the Government's request has varied, and while some have postponed rent increases, Birmingham City Council has refused to place the additional burden upon the ratepayers at large.

187. Rents paid for business premises and for land have, in the Government's view, an effect on prices that is strictly comparable with the impact on prices of goods and services. Landlords are exhorted to take this into account.

188. Local authorities are urged by the Government to encourage all proper economies in expenditure.

189. These principles for the voluntary freeze are easy to state and hard to apply in practice. It will only become clear in the course of time what the details of the policy are. Rents and rates cannot, it is thought, be brought within the early-warning and standstill provisions of sections 7 and 8 (see §§ 112–126), nor the statutory freeze provisions of sections 26 and 27 (see §§ 68–74). In other words they cannot be said to be either " prices for the sale of goods " or " charges for the performance of services ". They may of course be referred to the Prices and Incomes Board for report under the much wider provisions of section 2 (see § 102), but this does not in itself impose any statutory ban on increases.

190. Building Society mortgage interest.—The voluntary freeze has presented the Building Societies with a very difficult problem, which is likely to give trouble to the Government in carrying out its policy. The

---

* Now Schedule 2 to the Act (see § 104).

Building Societies were not inclined, as the Government wished, to put off for six months their proposed increase of interest rates to $7\frac{1}{8}$ per cent. as from 1st October next. They have to consider what effect this forbearance would have on their liquidity and reserve ratios; they cannot allow their financial positions to be jeopardised and they must be able to attract a sufficient inflow of funds to nourish an active lending policy. The Government has no power of compulsion in this matter, but tried to talk the Societies into agreement with its views—a difficult task, as exceptionally heavy pressure on the rates of Societies developed after the last increase of Bank Rate. Moreover some Government supporters hold that the building programme which figured so prominently in their election propaganda must at all costs be carried through. It cannot be unless the Building Societies can sustain their role of loan providers. This they may not be able to do for long. They are still attracting funds at an average gross interest rate of $6\frac{3}{4}$ per cent. but the inflow is drying up; competition for money has so intensified that sound and solid industrial companies are having to pay as much as 8 per cent. on well-secured debentures. And, if the Societies cannot borrow they obviously cannot lend. Building Society margins are certainly not sizable enough to absorb an increase of the rate at which the Societies borrow unless they can raise their lending rates.

191. Building Society mortgage interest rates, like rents and local rates, are for the reasons stated in § 189 not within the scope of any statutory control which could be applied to them. They may be, and indeed have been, referred to the Prices and Incomes Board for report under the much wider provisions of section 2 (see § 102), but this does not of itself impose any statutory ban on increases. This is in accordance with the view expressed by Mr. George Brown in Committee, when he stated that Building Society mortgage interest came within section 2 but not section 26, which he said " has nothing to do with mortgage interest rates or that kind of thing ". Confusion was caused by a hasty conclusion that since Building Society interest was not within the scope of the statutory freeze, it did not come within the voluntary freeze either. This is not the case, and on this as on many points the Government is asking for a much wider area of restraint than is covered by the legislation.

---

10. COMMENTS IN COMMITTEE

192. Hansard is always a rich mine of information and the House of Commons Official Reports on the Sittings of Standing Committee B provide additional background material which all interested in the Prices and Incomes Act should study.

193. Temporary and permanent provisions.—The first sitting of the Committee was on 26th July when Mr. George Brown carefully explained that Part I of the Bill was permanent, that Part II would be on the Statute Book permanently and could come into operation at the chosen time, and that a new Part IV, containing purely temporary provisions for temporary operation, would die at the end of the twelve month period for which its provisions were designed. That Part contained no powers at all for its resuscitation. It was made quite clear on this occasion that Conservative members of the Committee mistrusted the Bill, as it then was, but concentrated their dislike of the policies to which it gave legal expression on Part IV. And Part IV of the Act is still the area in which controversy rages.

194. Competition between Prices and Incomes Board and other statutory bodies.—The point was also made at this sitting that the establishing of the Prices and Incomes Board as a statutory body could lead to conflict with the Monopolies Commission and the Restrictive Practices Court, both organisations concerned in long-term policies and both requiring the services of highly skilled staffs and advisers. The Prices and Incomes Board will have equal need of expert advice and help. Where will it find it with so many other organisations busy investigating, inquiring, reporting and passing judgment?

195. As was asked earlier in this narrative, are there not too many Boards competing for skilled labour in a sparsely populated market, and does not this overcrowding cause wasteful duplication of effort? During last year's discussion on the Monopolies Bill the question of membership of the Monopolies Commission cropped up. The Board of Trade then stressed that there was a shortage of qualified people to serve on the Commission. It was mainly for this reason that the Commission could not be expanded to carry out its work more rapidly. What chance has the Prices and Incomes Board of attracting sufficient recruits of a calibre to ensure that the work likely to be piled upon it is dealt with efficiently and expeditiously?

196. That the Prices and Incomes Board should work in close association with the Board of Trade and other Government departments and with the N.E.D.C.'s and other advisory bodies was an idea that found general favour at the first sitting of Committee B. Others have suggested this move towards a closer relationship on various occasions but, so far, little seems to have been done to develop the idea. At present economists speak one language, lawyers another and accountants yet another and the general public is left mystified.

197. Lack of definitions.—At the second meeting of the Committee it was complained that many phrases used in the Bill were not as accurately defined as they might be. In support of this criticism a distinction was drawn between " capital invested " and " capital employed ", which most economists and accountants would understand but of which no account is taken by the legislature. The definitions in section 34 of the Act (see §§ 167–173) extend the meaning of certain words; for instance it provides that " ' goods ' includes ships and aircraft, minerals, substances and animals (including fish) ". But no explanation is given of many expressions which are presumed to bear their ordinary meaning, and the ordinary meaning of which is not clear.

198. As it stands the lack of clarity in the Act could impair the Board's usefulness when investigations are being made, or reports prepared or comparisons drawn. In no field of legislation is absolute clarity of wording more needed than in legislation which has as its subject matter the complex affairs of the business community.

199. Another problem of definition would have arisen had an amendment been accepted to include notification of " net profits " as well as " distributions " in section 12. The accountancy profession itself gives many meanings to that apparently simple word " profits ", and has not adopted a standard terminology.

200. It has been one purpose of this narrative to try to explain the meaning of the Act in " layman's language ", but only the actual words of the Act have the force of law, and even if the Government issues a booklet reducing the legal phraseology of the Act to simple and understandable terms, it will only be a guide without legal authority.

201. The need for statistics.—The lack of reliable statistics was another point taken up and discussed in Committee. A Conservative member of the Committee stated that, from official answers given him, he gathered that, though an estimated 611,600 persons were engaged in the catering trade, no information on earnings was available. He had been told that although 2,961,900 persons were employed in the distributive trades, the estimate of earnings was based on a small household sample. He was told that no information was available on earnings in the cinema, fishing, forestry and sport and recreation trades. No Act of the importance of the Prices and Incomes Act can be considered complete if its provisions are based on an inadequate information service and no Board can properly conduct its affairs unless it has at its disposal a readily available store of reliable statistics.

202. One speaker slightingly referred to the " guestimates " of the original Schedule 2 (General Considerations relating to Prices and Incomes). He very properly pointed out that the sums used and on which the National Plan was based were out of date. The Plan was now a dream; the figures it displayed were tired and could seriously mislead. The Schedule has now been altered as described in § 104.

203. This criticism was taken up by another Committee member who had this to say: " In seeking to establish some kind of future trend for national productivity, one must examine the Government's statistical service. There are so many gaps that, in Ministry after Ministry, the civil servants are involved in making forecasts which are no more than guesses. They have to fill in the gaps without knowledge they ought to have. There are gaps also in the statistics coming forward from industry and the trade unions. I doubt that more than half of British industry collects the figures which are required or passes them forward to the Board of Trade or the Ministry of Labour. If figures are secured from only half the industry there will inevitably be variations in the final figure, and this will lead to mistakes which will in turn affect the kind of forecast one tries to make for productivity, manpower or national economic development." Improvement of our statistical services can wait awhile but the process should not be long delayed.

204. Advisory panels.—The Chairman of the Prices and Wages Board may require preliminary consideration by three members of the Board with members of the panels of employers and employees. It was unsuccessfully urged in Committee that a panel of consumers should also be available. True it would be difficult, but not impossible, to decide what bodies could best present the views of consumers.

205. Dictatorial powers?—Quite early in the debate, on Part IV, Mr. Brown disarmed, or attempted to disarm, criticism that the Prices and Incomes Act would confer powers on the Government more suited to a dictatorship than to a democracy. He referred to subsection (2) of section 25 of the Act (the opening section of Part IV), and confirmed that this section did not, of itself, give the Government any new powers. It had, he went on, two main purposes. First, it provided that the various powers listed in Part IV should be subject to the requirement of an affirmative Resolution by Parliament within 28 days, and secondly that all these powers will entirely lapse one year after the Royal Assent. Again Mr. Brown officially praised the virtues of a discipline not enforced but resting on voluntary support. Mr. Brown's honeyed explanations did not, of course, satisfy a sceptical opposition. Nor did the attempt to hide that there were difficulties lying ahead of those charged with the carrying out of the Prices and Incomes Policy.

206. A " voluntary " system?—Mr. Brown referred to the " standstill " arrangements outlined in paragraph 9 of the latest White Paper* (Cmnd. 3073, dealing with the overall price freeze). This paragraph laid down that any manufacturing enterprise (with certain stated exceptions) which considered it would be justified in proposing a price increase would have to notify the appropriate Government Department. It went on to say that an enterprise applying for permission to increase its prices was not expected to make any such increase unless it had received

---

* Now Schedule 2 to the Act (see § 104).

written confirmation from the Government that no further standstill on the increase was required. This period of waiting is voluntary at the moment, but is covered by section 26. The Government will not, however, use those compulsory powers except as a last resort.

207. No price standstill can, of course, be made to work without difficulty, but, again to quote Mr. Brown: " Whether there is a compulsory or voluntary basis . . . difficulties will have to be worked out, but the more we work on the voluntary basis we will find acceptable answers ". The nation must hope that the First Secretary's faith in the voluntary system is not broken when the full rigours of the standstill and severe restraint period are encountered.

208. Mr. Brown's insistence that he was going to rely on the voluntary principle was, indeed, described by one of his most persistent questioners as " mere sophistry ". The voluntary system went, he said, when the Prices and Incomes Bill became an Act. And so, to some extent, it did. A voluntary system can work only if possible absentees from its ranks are persuaded by threat of punishment into good behaviour. Mr. Brown did seem, during much of the Committee's debating, " to mix up his philosophy with his law ", as a committee member put it. " Speak softly and wave a big stick ", Theodore Roosevelt once said, a dictum of which Mr. Brown and, indeed, all in positions of authority would, on occasions tacitly approve.

---

11. CONCLUSIONS

209. Will the Government's anti-inflation policies work? They will work if these policies are grimly adhered to by the Government and if the nation as a whole is willing to make the necessary sacrifices and to exercise the necessary restraints. The reactions of foreign countries to the austerity programme initiated by Mr. Wilson on 20th July have varied. The severity of that programme has at least convinced Europe and America that we mean business. On 20th July, it will be recalled, the Prime Minister unfolded a retrenchment programme designed, in one way or another, to bring down claims on the domestic economy by more than £500 million and to reduce overseas spending, private and public, by as much as £150 million; this on top of earlier budgetary measures which lowered pressure of demand in the private sector of the economy by some £700 million. At the same time Mr. Wilson gave detail of a proposed six-month standstill on wages, salaries and other forms of income, of a similar prices standstill and of a 12-month period of dividend restraint. In addition a 10 per cent. surcharge was levied on purchase tax and excise duties, foreign travel allowances were cut and surtax was raised by 10 per cent. for one year. Building controls were tightened up, demands on public investment are to be reduced by £150 million in 1967–68, central and local Government will be cut by £55 million in that year. Investment by the nationalised industries will be reduced by £95 million, and certain postal charges are being increased.

210. The U.S.A. gave a specially warm welcome to this proof of British determination to beat inflation and to give confidence to sterling. A Washington Treasury Statement of 20th July said this: " The actions taken are strong and far-reaching; they go further than any measures taken over the past few years. They strike at the core of the internal inflationary pressures in the U.K. and should effectively promote the objectives of sterling stability and balance payments equilibrium." Zurich, home of the famous gnomes, was less enthusiastic and expressed the opinion that still sterner measures should have been taken. Paris, too, was doubtful but Bonn was pleased that the U.K. Government had deliberately chosen to deflate the economy and had shown itself prepared to incur unpopularity in pursuit of that objective.

211. It had been hoped that sterling would gain considerably in strength on the foreign bourses in response to the action taken by the Government. It did not do so with quite the vigour expected. Sterling has, in fact, fluctuated and fears of possible devaluation linger. If the Prices and Incomes Act fails to achieve what it has set out to do some form of sterling devaluation could, of course, become necessary.

212. Informed reaction at home to the Government's anti-inflation measures has been and remains critical. Economists and writers generally agree that Mr. Wilson's policy of deflation should in 1967 put an end to our balance of payment difficulties but the continuing need to support sterling has puzzled commentators. It may well be that foreign centres are not yet entirely convinced that our prices and incomes policy will be successfully carried through and maintained in full severity against popular outcry.

213. The crisis has or should have taught the nation a hard lesson in elementary economics. But how many people fully understand what caused the crisis, and how many can say that they fully understand the purport of the Prices and Incomes Act? This public lack of interest in and understanding of finance is a deficiency disease for which a cure must be sought and applied. The public needs to be educated and the present crisis should have persuaded many that the crisis would not have occurred or would certainly have been less severe had more people been aware of the deterioration that was taking place in the economy of the United Kingdom. Had that been so counter-measures would have been taken by the Government at an earlier date than July 1966. For this failure of communication between Government and people both

are to blame. The Government has not, even yet, really taken the nation into its confidence or really troubled to. And it launched the Prices and Incomes Act upon the nation in its raw indigestable state with hardly a word of explanation.

214. Quite recently the third International Convention of Investment Clubs was held in London. It took as its subject " Investment Education ". Mr. George A. Nicholson, Chairman of the Board of Advisors to the U.S. National Association of Investment Clubs spoke at the Convention and agreed that the movement was a catalyst that could bring together Government, industry and the financial community for the common purpose of investment education. Some such education is much needed in this country, a point emphasised by another speaker at the Convention, Mr. R. J. Clark, economic adviser to the West-minster Bank. Mr. Clark said that, though it would be wrong to attribute all our present ills to economic ignorance, there was little doubt but that a higher level of economic literacy would have enabled Britain to manage her affairs more competently than she has done. Every convenient agency should be used, he added, to make people aware of the economic facts of life. Had there been such agencies at work in this country there might have been no long crisis culminating in the Prices and Income Act 1966. That this need for a broader and more accurate knowledge of the nation's working economy is being increasingly recognised in Britain was made evident by the many appeals made for a better service of statistics by many speakers during the committee stage of the Act, to which reference has already been made in this narrative. But Government moves slowly in these matters. It is some years since the late Sir Stafford Cripps suggested that the Budget should be set out in a simpler form, understandable to all, but it is still presented each year in its traditional and now archaic make-up. Something will no doubt be done, some time. The study of economics may even, in time, become commonplace in every sixth-form curriculum and for every Member of Parliament, for every officer of a trade union, for every shop steward and for every member of a Board of Directors.

THE PRICES AND INCOMES ACT 1966

(1966 c. 33)

ARRANGEMENT OF SECTIONS

PART I

THE NATIONAL BOARD FOR PRICES AND INCOMES

PART II

NOTICES AND STANDSTILLS

General

Prices and charges

Company distributions

Terms and conditions of employment

[*1*]

[2]

An Act to establish a National Board for Prices and Incomes, and authorise the bringing into force of provisions requiring notice of price increases, pay increases and other matters, and for enforcing a temporary standstill in prices or charges or terms and conditions of employment; in connection with recommendations made by the said Board, to amend the Restrictive Trade Practices Act 1956; to provide, for a period lasting not more than twelve months, for restricting price increases and pay increases and for other matters connected with prices and incomes; and for connected purposes.

[12th August 1966]

PART I

THE NATIONAL BOARD FOR PRICES AND INCOMES

1. Constitution and proceedings of the Board.—(1) There shall be established a body, to be called the National Board for Prices and Incomes (in this Act referred to as " the Board ").

(2) Subject to subsection (6) below, the Board shall consist of not less than nine and not more than fifteen members appointed by the Secretary of State.

(3) The Secretary of State may appoint persons to the Board either as full-time members or as part-time members.

(4) Of the full-time members, the Secretary of State shall appoint one to be chairman of the Board and one or more, as he thinks fit, to be deputy chairman or deputy chairmen.

(5) The Secretary of State shall, out of money provided by Parliament—

(a) pay to the members of the Board such remuneration, and such travelling or other allowances, as he may with the approval of the Treasury determine, and

(b) in the case of any member of the Board to whom he may, with the approval of the Treasury, determine that this paragraph applies, pay such pension, allowance or gratuity to or in respect of the member on his retirement or death, or make such payments towards the provision of such a pension, allowance or gratuity, as he may, with the like approval, determine;

and if a person ceases to be a member of the Board and it appears to the Secretary of State that there are special circumstances which make it right that that person should receive compensation, he may, with the approval of the Treasury, pay to that person out of money provided by Parliament a sum of such amount as he may with the approval of the Treasury determine.

(6) The Secretary of State may, by an order contained in a statutory instrument subject to annulment in pursuance of a resolution of either House of Parliament—

(*a*) direct that the minimum or maximum number of members of the Board shall be a number greater or less than that specified in subsection (2) above;

(*b*) vary or revoke any previous order containing such a direction.

(7) The provisions of Schedule 1 to this Act shall have effect with respect to the Board, its members, officers and servants and proceedings.

NATIONAL BOARD FOR PRICES AND INCOMES
This Board was originally appointed by H.M. the Queen by Royal Warrant, which provided, *inter alia*, for its membership and terms of reference. The Chairman of the Board is the Rt. Hon. Aubrey Jones.
Further provisions relating to the Board are contained, in particular, in ss. 2–5 and Schs. 1 and 2, *post*.

STATUTORY INSTRUMENT SUBJECT TO ANNULMENT
Provisions as to statutory instruments generally are contained in the Statutory Instruments Act 1946 (24 Halsbury's Statutes (2nd Edn.) 440). As to statutory instruments which are subject to annulment, see ss. 5 (1) and 7 (1) of that Act (24 Halsbury's Statutes (2nd Edn.) 443, 445).

ORDERS UNDER THIS SECTION
No order had been made under sub-s. (6) up to 15th August 1966.

2. References of questions to the Board.—(1) The Secretary of State, or the Secretary of State and any other Minister acting jointly, may refer to the Board any question relating to wages, salaries or other forms of incomes, or to prices, charges or other sums payable under transactions of any description relating to any form of property or rights or to services of any description or to returns on capital invested in any form of property, including company dividends; and without prejudice to the generality of the foregoing provisions of this subsection the Secretary of State, or the Secretary of State and any other Minister acting jointly, may refer to the Board any question—

(*a*) relating to a proposal to increase any prices for the sale of goods or any charges for the performance of services, including charges for the application of any process to goods, or

(*b*) relating to any pay claims or other claims relating to terms and conditions of employment, or any awards and settlements relating to terms and conditions of employment.

(2) A question referred to the Board under subsection (1) above may be framed in any way whatsoever, and in particular may be concerned with a specified region or locality or with named undertakings or persons.

(3) The Minister or Ministers referring any question to the Board under this section may at any time by a further reference to the Board vary or withdraw that question.

(4) The text of any reference under subsection (1) or subsection (3) above shall be published in the Gazette.

(5) The Board shall examine any question referred to them under this section and report to the Minister or Ministers who referred the question to the Board.

REFER TO THE BOARD ANY QUESTION, ETC.
For the consequences of certain references to the Board under sub-s. (1) or (3) of this section, see ss. 7 (3) (*b*), 8 (1), 14 (6) (*b*) and 15 (1), *post*; and as to the obtaining of information regarding increases in company distributions to assist the Secretary of State and other Ministers to determine whether any question concerning any company or companies should be referred to the Board under this section, see s. 12, *post*.

SALE OF GOODS
This Act applies to conditional sale agreements and hire-purchase agreements in accordance with s. 34 (3), *post*.

SHALL EXAMINE ANY QUESTION
As to the principles to be applied by the Board in examining any question referred under this section, see s. 4 and Sch. 2, *post*; and as to the remission of questions for preliminary examination by groups of members and persons specially appointed, see s. 1 (7), *ante*, and Sch. 1, paras. 10–12, *post*.

REPORT TO THE MINISTER
As to the Board's reports, see s. 5, *post*.

DEFINITIONS
For " the Board ", see s. 1 (1), *ante*; for " awards and settlements ", " goods ", " Minister " and " price ", see s. 34 (1), *post*; for " Gazette ", see s. 34 (4), *post*.

3. Instructions to Board to keep certain prices or incomes under continuous review.—(1) The Secretary of State may by order apply this section to any incomes or prices or charges or other matters which may be the subject of a reference under the last foregoing section.

(2) The Secretary of State, or the Secretary of State and any other Minister acting jointly, may instruct the Board to keep under continuous review any question concerning all or any of the incomes or prices or charges or other matters to which this section applies.

(3) The Board shall from time to time, as the Board thinks fit, report to the Minister or Ministers giving any instruction under this section on the matters to which the instruction relates; and the Secretary of State, or the Secretary of State and any other Minister acting jointly, may at any time require the Board to make to the Minister or Ministers imposing the requirement a report on those matters, or on any question relating to them.

(4) The Minister or Ministers giving an instruction to the Board under this section may at any time vary or withdraw it by a further instruction.

(5) The text of any instruction under subsection (2) or subsection (4) above shall be published in the Gazette.

(6) An order or instruction under this section may be framed in any way whatsoever, and in particular may be concerned with a specified region or locality or with named undertakings or persons.

(7) An order made under subsection (1) of this section—

(*a*) may be varied or revoked by a subsequent order so made,

(*b*) shall be made by statutory instrument subject to annulment in pursuance of a resolution of either House of Parliament.

(8) The powers conferred by this section are in addition to, and not in derogation of, the powers conferred by the last foregoing section.

INSTRUCT THE BOARD; REQUIRE THE BOARD
As to the principles which are to be applied by the Board in complying with any instruction or requirement under this section, see s. 4 and Sch. 2, *post*; and as to the remission of matters for preliminary examination by groups of members and persons specially appointed, see s. 1 (7), *ante*, and Sch. 1, paras. 10–12, *post*.
By s. 12, *post*, provision is made relating to the obtaining of information regarding increases in company distributions to assist the Secretary of State and other Ministers to determine whether any instruction or requirement should be given to or imposed on the Board under this section.

REPORT TO THE MINISTER
As to the Board's reports, see s. 5, *post*.

STATUTORY INSTRUMENT SUBJECT TO ANNULMENT
See the note to s. 1, *ante*.

DEFINITIONS
For " the Board ", see s. 1 (1), *ante*; for " Minister " and " price ", see s. 34 (1), *post*; for " Gazette ", see s. 34 (4), *post*.

ORDERS UNDER THIS SECTION
No order had been made under sub-s. (1) up to 15th August 1966.

4. Principles to be applied by the Board.—(1) In examining any question referred to the Board under section 2 above, and in complying with any instruction or requirement under section 3 above, the Board shall, subject to the following provisions of this section, have regard to the considerations set out in Schedule 2 to this Act (which reproduces Part I of a memorandum presented to Parliament by the Secretary of State by Command of Her Majesty in April 1965).

(2) The Secretary of State may at any time by order set out considerations to which the Board are to have regard under this section whether in addition to, or by way of variation of or substitution for, the considerations set out in Schedule 2 to this Act.

(3) Before making an order under subsection (2) above the Secretary of State shall consult such organisations or bodies as he thinks fit, being organisations or bodies which appear to him to represent to any substantial extent the interests of those particularly concerned with the order, and any order so made—

(*a*)   may be varied or revoked by a subsequent order so made,

(*b*)   shall be made by statutory instrument subject to annulment in pursuance of a resolution of either House of Parliament:

Provided that in the period of six months beginning with the passing of this Act an order may be made under subsection (2) above without any prior consultation as required by the foregoing provisions of this subsection.

THE BOARD
I.e., The National Board for Prices and Incomes; see s. 1 (1), *ante.*

MEMORANDUM PRESENTED TO PARLIAMENT. . . BY COMMAND OF HER MAJESTY IN APRIL 1965
This was Command Paper No. 2639, entitled "Prices and Incomes Policy". Part I of that Command Paper is reproduced in Sch. 2, *post.* Part II dealt with the appointment by Royal Warrant and membership, etc. of the National Board for Prices and Incomes, which Board is now given statutory authority by s. 1, *ante.*

CONSULT
As to what constitutes consultation, see *Rollo* v. *Minister of Town and Country Planning,* [1948] 1 All E.R. 13, C.A., and *Re Union of Whippingham and East Cowes Benefices, Derham* v. *Church Comrs. of England,* [1954] 2 All E.R. 22; [1954] A.C. 245, P.C.

STATUTORY INSTRUMENT SUBJECT TO ANNULMENT
See the note to s. 1, *ante.*

PASSING OF THIS ACT
This Act was passed (*i.e.,* received the Royal Assent) on 12th August 1966.

ORDERS UNDER THIS SECTION
The Secretary of State has, by order under sub-s. (2), substituted a new Sch. 2, which reproduces the memorandum entitled "Prices and Incomes Standstill" (Cmnd. 3073), which was presented to Parliament in July 1966.

5.   The Board's reports.—(1) The Minister or Ministers concerned shall lay any report made by the Board in pursuance of section 2 or section 3 above before each House of Parliament, shall publish it in such manner as appears to the Minister or Ministers to be appropriate, and shall record in the Gazette the date on which it is first so published; and that date shall be taken as the date of publication for the purposes of this Act.

(2) If it appears to the Minister or Ministers concerned that the publication of any matter in the report would be against the interests of national security, the Minister or Ministers shall exclude that matter from the copies of the report laid before Parliament and published under the foregoing subsection.

(3) Subject to subsection (4) below—

(*a*) any report of the Board under section 2 above must be published under subsection (1) above within three months from the date on which the reference (meaning, if the original reference has been varied by a reference under section 2(3) above, the original reference) is published in the Gazette, and

(*b*) any report of the Board in compliance with the requirement of a Minister or Ministers under section 3(3) of this Act must be published under subsection (1) above within three months from the date when the requirement was imposed,

and it shall be the duty of the Board to make their report so as to allow publication within the time limited by this subsection.

(4) The Minister or Ministers concerned may by a direction published in the Gazette extend or further extend the period of three months mentioned in paragraph (*a*) or paragraph (*b*) of the last foregoing subsection by such further period as is specified in the direction.

(5) In framing any report the Board shall have regard to the need for excluding, so far as that is practicable, matter which relates to the private affairs of any person and the publication of which would or might in the opinion of the Board prejudicially affect the interests of that person.

(6) For the purposes of the law relating to defamation absolute privilege shall attach to any report of the Board.

(7) In this section " the Minister or Ministers concerned ", in relation to any report of the Board, means the Minister or Ministers to whom the report is to be made.

LAY BEFORE... PARLIAMENT...
For meaning, see the Laying of Documents before Parliament (Interpretation) Act 1948, s. 1 (1) (24 Halsbury's Statutes (2nd Edn.) 448).

WITHIN THREE MONTHS
In calculating this period the date on which the reference was published in the Gazette, or when the requirement was imposed, is not to be included; see, in particular, *Goldsmiths' Co. v. West Metropolitan Rail. Co.*, [1904] 1 K.B. 1; [1900–03] All E.R. Rep. 667, C.A.; *Stewart v. Chapman*, [1951] 2 All E.R. 613; [1951] 2 K.B. 792; and *Cartwright v. MacCormack (Trafalgar Insurance Co., Ltd., Third Parties)*, [1963] 1 All E.R. 11, C.A. " Months " means calendar months by virtue of the Interpretation Act 1889, s. 3 (24 Halsbury's Statutes (2nd Edn.) 207).

Under s. 19 (1), *post*, if the report of the Board on a question referred to them under s. 2 (1), *ante*, is not published by a date within three months from the publication of the reference certain specified provisions in Part II of this Act are to apply as if the report had been so published on the last day of that period.

DATE ON WHICH THE REFERENCE... IS PUBLISHED IN THE GAZETTE
This is to be construed in accordance with s. 34 (4), *post*. The reference is required to be so published by s. 2 (4), *ante*.

ABSOLUTE PRIVILEGE SHALL ATTACH TO ANY REPORT
The effect of sub-s. (6) is that no action for defamation will lie against the
Board. As to absolute privilege generally, see 24 Halsbury's Laws (3rd Edn.)
48 *et seq.*

MINISTER . . . TO WHOM ITS REPORT IS TO BE MADE
I.e., in accordance with s. 2 (5) or 3 (3), *ante.*

DEFINITIONS
For " the Board ", see s. 1 (1), *ante*; for " Minister ", see s. 34 (1), *post*;
for " Gazette ", see s. 34 (4), *post.* Note as to " the Minister or Ministers concerned ", sub-s. (7) of this section.

PART II

NOTICES AND STANDSTILLS

General

6. Power to bring Part II into force.—(1) Her Majesty may by Order
in Council of which a draft has been laid before and approved by a
resolution of each House of Parliament—

(*a*) bring the provisions of this Part of this Act into force for a
   period of twelve months beginning with the date specified
   in the Order,

(*b*) from time to time extend or further extend that period by a
   further period of twelve months,

and if the Secretary of State proposes to lay a draft of an Order in
Council under this subsection before Parliament he shall first consult
with such organisations or bodies as he thinks fit, being organisations
or bodies which appear to him to represent to any substantial extent
the interests of those particularly concerned with the Order.

(2) The provisions which may be so brought into force may be all
the following sections in this Part of this Act, or all of them except
7 to 12, or all of them except 13 to 18.

(3) If an Order in Council brings this Part of this Act into force
without either of those groups of sections a further Order in Council
under subsection (1) above may bring into force that group of sections
(together with the other sections of this Part of this Act as they apply
for the purposes of any of that group of sections) for the residue of the
period for which the remainder of this Part of this Act is in force, or
for a different period of twelve months which may be separately extended
under subsection (1)(*b*) above.

(4) Without prejudice to the provisions of section 37 of the Interpretation Act 1889 (power to make subordinate legislation in advance
of coming into force of an Act), any power of making orders under the
following provisions of this Part of this Act may be exercised before
those provisions are brought into force on any occasion, but not so as to
have any effect before they are so brought into force.

[*9*]

(5) Her Majesty may by Order in Council at any time revoke an Order in Council made under subsection (1) above.

(6) The lapse of provisions of this Part of this Act on the expiration of a period specified in an Order in Council under subsection (1) above, or on the revocation of such an Order in Council, shall not affect liability for any offence committed before the lapse, and shall be without prejudice to the further exercise of the powers conferred by subsection (1)(*a*) above.

LAID BEFORE ... PARLIAMENT
For meaning, see the Laying of Documents before Parliament (Interpretation) Act 1948, s. 1 (1) (24 Halsbury's Statutes (2nd Edn.) 448).

TWELVE MONTHS BEGINNING WITH THE DATE, ETC.
See the note " Thirty days beginning with the date, etc." to s. 7, *post.*

CONSULT
See the note to s. 4, *ante.*

INTERPRETATION ACT 1889, S. 37
See 24 Halsbury's Statutes (2nd Edn.) 228.

ORDERS IN COUNCIL UNDER THIS SECTION
No Order in Council had been made under this section, bringing this Part into force, up to 15th August 1966.
The powers to make Orders in Council are exercisable by statutory instrument; see the Statutory Instruments Act 1946, s. 1 (1) (24 Halsbury's Statutes (2nd Edn.) 441).

Prices and Charges

7. Notice of intention to increase prices or charges.—(1) The Secretary of State may by order apply this section to any prices for the sale of goods and to any charges for the performance of services, including charges for the application of any process to goods.

(2) Prices or charges to which this section applies shall not be increased by any amount unless notice of intention to increase them by at least that amount has been duly given to the appropriate Minister.

(3) When notice of intention to increase prices or charges to which this section applies has been duly given to the appropriate Minister—

(*a*) those prices shall not be increased until after the expiration of a period of thirty days beginning with the date on which that notice of intention is so given, except that if at any earlier time the person giving that notice of intention receives written notice from the said Minister stating that it has been decided not to refer the notice of intention to the Board, this paragraph shall apply only until that earlier time,

(*b*) if under section 2(1) or 2(3) of this Act the notice of intention is referred to the Board by a reference published in the Gazette within the said period of thirty days, those prices or charges shall not without the written consent of the Minister or Ministers who referred the notice be increased until the date of publication of the Board's report on the reference.

[*10*]

Any written consent given under paragraph (*b*) above shall be notified in the Gazette.

(4) An order under subsection (1) above may frame a description of prices or charges to which this section applies in any way, and in particular in framing a description of prices of goods of a specified class—

(*a*) may make distinctions by reference to the undertakings or persons selling the goods,

(*b*) may make distinctions by reference to the terms and conditions on which the goods are sold, the quantity sold or the undertakings or persons to whom they are sold,

(*c*) may make distinctions by reference to the undertakings or persons by whom the goods have been produced or dealt with, or the locality in which they have been produced,

(*d*) in making any of the distinctions above as regards undertakings or persons, may distinguish undertakings or persons by reference to the regions or localities where they carry on business or the scale or turnover of their business or by reference to any other circumstances, and may include or exclude named undertakings or named persons;

and comparable distinctions may be made in relation to charges for the performance of services.

(5) An order under subsection (1) above may provide for the manner in which account is to be taken of any discount allowed in any transaction and may be applied both to any price before discount is allowed and also to any price after allowance of discount.

BRINGING OF THIS PART INTO FORCE
> See s. 6, *ante*.

SALE OF GOODS
> This Act applies to conditional sale agreements and hire-purchase agreements in accordance with s. 34 (3), *post*.

SHALL NOT BE INCREASED
> As to whether prices charged or charges made represent an increase, see s. 10, *post*; and as to offences and the punishment thereof, see s. 11, *post*.

NOTICE OF INTENTION...HAS BEEN DULY GIVEN TO THE APPROPRIATE MINISTER
> The giving of notices is to be governed by regulations made under s. 21, *post*.

THIRTY DAYS BEGINNING WITH THE DATE, ETC.
> In calculating the period of thirty days the day upon which notice of intention is given must be included; see *Hare* v. *Gocher*, [1962] 2 All E.R. 763; [1962] 2 Q.B. 641.

WRITTEN
> By the Interpretation Act 1889, s. 20 (24 Halsbury's Statutes (2nd Edn.) 222), expressions referring to writing include any mode of representing or reproducing words in a visible form.

PUBLISHED IN THE GAZETTE WITHIN THE SAID PERIOD OF THIRTY DAYS
> As to the date of publication in the Gazette, see s. 34 (4), *post*.

[*11*]

DATE OF PUBLICATION OF THE BOARD'S REPORT
As to this date, see s. 5 (1), *ante.* By s. 19 (1), *post,* if the report of the Board on a question referred to the Board under s. 2 (1), *ante,* is not published in accordance with the said s. 5 (1) by a date within three months from the publication of the reference, sub-s. (3) (*b*) of the section is to apply as if the report had been so published on the last day of that period; see also s. 19 (2), *post,* as to the application of sub-s. (3) (*b*) in relation to interim or partial reports.

SUPPLEMENTAL PROVISIONS
See s. 9, *post.*

DEFINITIONS
For " the Board ", see s. 1 (1), *ante*; for " appropriate Minister ", " goods", "Minister" and "price ", see s. 34 (1), *post*; for " Gazette ", see s. 34 (4), *post.*

ORDERS UNDER THE SECTION
No order had been made under sub-s. (1) up to 15th August 1966.
For general provisions as to orders made under this Part of the Act, see s. 20, *post,* and s. 6 (4), *ante*; and for supplemental provisions as to orders under this section, see s. 9 (1), *post.*

8. Standstill for prices or charges referred to Board.—(1) If under section 2(1) or 2(3) of this Act any question is referred to the Board concerning prices for the sale of goods or charges for the performance of services, including charges for the application of any process to goods, the Secretary of State, or the Secretary of State acting jointly with any other Minister, may by notice published in the issue of the Gazette in which the text of the reference is published direct that this section shall apply to such prices or charges as may be specified in the direction, being matters to which the reference relates.

(2) Prices or charges to which this section applies shall not be increased until the date of publication of the Board's report on the reference, except that if at any earlier time the direction under subsection (1) above is revoked in whole or in part by notice published in the Gazette by the Minister or Ministers who gave the direction this subsection shall apply, or as the case may be shall apply to matters affected by the partial revocation, only until that earlier time.

BRINGING OF THIS PART INTO FORCE
See s. 6, *ante.*

SALE OF GOODS
This Act applies to conditional sale agreements and hire-purchase agreements in accordance with s. 34 (3), *post.*

TEXT OF THE REFERENCE IS PUBLISHED
I.e., under s. 2 (4), *ante.*

SHALL NOT BE INCREASED
As to whether prices charged or charges made represent an increase, see s. 10, *post*; and as to offences and the punishment thereof, see s. 11, *post.*

DATE OF PUBLICATION OF THE BOARD'S REPORT
As to this date, see s. 5 (1), *ante.* By virtue of s. 19 (1), *post,* if the report of the Board on a question referred to them under s. 2 (1), *ante,* is not published in accordance with the said s. 5 (1) by a date within three months from the

publication of the reference this section is to apply as if the report had been so published on the last day of that period; see also s. 19 (2), *post*, as to the application of this section in relation to interim or partial reports.

SUPPLEMENTAL PROVISIONS
    See s. 9, *infra*.

DEFINITIONS
    For " the Board ", see s. 1 (1), *ante*; for " goods ", " Minister " and " price ", see s. 34 (1), *post*; for " Gazette ", see s. 34 (4), *post*.

9. Prices and charges: supplemental provisions.—(1) An order under section 7 of this Act, and a direction under section 8 of this Act, shall contain such provisions for excluding prices and charges as appear to the Minister or Ministers making the order or giving the direction practicable and appropriate for the purpose of ensuring that those sections do not impede export trade (that is to say the provision of goods and services for persons not resident in the United Kingdom).

(2) The provisions of Schedule 3 to this Act shall have effect for the purpose of excluding, wholly or partially, from the operation of the said sections 7 and 8 certain prices and charges which are subject to regulation under other enactments and, in connection with the regulation of which, the considerations referred to in section 4 of this Act are, subject to certain exceptions, applied by section 23 thereof.

(3) The said sections 7 and 8 shall not apply in relation to prices paid on any sale by auction.

(4) A transaction shall not be invalid because it involves a price or charge which contains a price increase forbidden by this Part of this Act but the person paying the price or charge shall be entitled to recover the amount representing that price increase unless he is a person who is himself liable to punishment by reason of his having aided, abetted, counselled or procured the offence committed under this Part of this Act by the other party to the transaction.

(5) The said sections 7 and 8 shall not apply in relation to a transaction effected in pursuance of a contract enforceable in law and concluded before the relevant price or charge was brought within section 7 of this Act by an order under that section or, as the case may be, before the direction was given under section 8 of this Act.

BRINGING OF THIS PART INTO FORCE
    See s. 6, *ante*.

UNITED KINGDOM
    This means Great Britain and Northern Ireland; see the Royal and Parliamentary Titles Act 1927, s. 2 (2) (4 Halsbury's Statutes (2nd Edn,) 192). The Channel Islands and the Isle of Man are not within this term.

PRICE INCREASE FORBIDDEN BY THIS PART
    I.e., by s. 7 (2) or (3) (*a*) or (*b*) or s. 8 (2), *ante*; see also s. 11 (3), *post*.

AIDED, ABETTED, COUNSELLED OR PROCURED THE OFFENCE... UNDER THIS PART

A person who aids, abets, counsels or procures the commission of such an offence (*i.e.*, an offence under s. 11 (1), *infra*) may be proceeded against as if he were a principal offender under the Accessories and Abettors Act 1861, s. 8 (5 Halsbury's Statutes (2nd Edn.) 726), or the Magistrates' Courts Act 1952, s. 35 (32 Halsbury's Statutes (2nd Edn.) 451).

DEFINITIONS

For " goods ", " Minister " and " price ", see s. 34 (1), *post*.

10. Comparison of prices and charges.—(1) In ascertaining for the purposes of this Part of this Act whether a price charged or quoted by any person represents an increase (that is to say as compared with prices charged or quoted at or for earlier times) the following provisions of this section shall have effect for selecting the prices to be taken for comparison.

(2) The price shall be compared with those charged or quoted by that person in the course of business for comparable transactions as regards goods of the same description.

(3) If there are no prices which can be taken for comparison under subsection (2) above the comparison may be with prices charged or quoted by that person in the course of business for transactions which are not in all respects comparable, and as regards goods which are not of precisely the same description, with a fair adjustment to take account of the differences.

As between different transactions or different descriptions of goods those taken for comparison under this subsection shall be those which are most closely comparable.

(4) In this section references to a price quoted by a person are references to a price at which that person offers to sell goods, or at which he gives notice of intention to do business by any display, advertisement, circular or other public notice.

(5) All the provisions of this section shall apply in relation to the performance of services as they apply in relation to the sale of goods, and references to prices charged or quoted shall, in this section as so applied, be construed as references to charges made or quoted.

BRINGING OF THIS PART INTO FORCE
See s. 6, *ante*.

OFFERS TO SELL
See the note " Offer to sell " to s. 11, *post*.

DEFINITIONS
For " business ", " goods " and " price ", see s. 34 (1), *post*. Note as to " price quoted ", sub-s. (4) of this section.

11. Prices and charges: enforcement.—(1) It shall be an offence for any person in the course of business—

[*14*]

(*a*) to sell, agree to sell or offer to sell any goods, or

(*b*) to perform, agree to perform or offer to perform any services,

if the price or charge for the goods or services represents an increase which is forbidden by the foregoing provisions of this Part of this Act.

(2) It shall be an offence for any person to give public notice of his intention to ask or make a price or charge which represents an increase which is forbidden by the foregoing provisions of this Part of this Act.

(3) For the purposes of this Act an increase contained in a price or charge is one which is forbidden by the foregoing provisions of this Part of this Act—

(*a*) if the sale of the goods or the performance of the services is to be effected at a time when the increase is forbidden,

(*b*) in the case of an agreement or offer to sell goods or perform services, if the agreement or offer is made at a time when the increase is forbidden, and the terms of the offer or agreement do not preclude the sale of the goods or performance of the services being effected at a time when the increase is forbidden,

(*c*) in the case of a public notice of intention to ask or make a price or charge, if the public notice is given at a time when the increase is forbidden, and the terms of the notice do not expressly exclude a sale of goods or performance of services at a time when the increase is forbidden,

and in ascertaining whether a price or charge represents an increase which is forbidden by the foregoing provisions of this Part of this Act there shall not be taken for comparison any other price or charge which represents such a forbidden increase.

(4) It shall be a defence to proceedings under subsection (1) or subsection (2) of this section for the accused person to show that in a comparable transaction effected in the ordinary course of business at a time before prices or charges of the description comprising that to which the proceedings relate were brought within section 7 of this Act by an order under that section or, as the case may be, before a direction was given under section 8 of this Act, he asked or made a price or charge not less than that to which the proceedings relate; and subsections (3) and (5) of the last foregoing section shall apply for effecting a comparison under this subsection between transactions which are not in all respects comparable.

(5) A person guilty of an offence under this section shall be liable—

(*a*) on summary conviction to a fine not exceeding one hundred pounds, and

(*b*) on conviction on indictment to a fine which, if the offender is not a body corporate, shall not exceed five hundred pounds.

BRINGING OF THIS PART INTO FORCE
See s. 6, *ante*.

IT SHALL BE AN OFFENCE
General provisions as to offences under this Part are contained in s. 22, *post*; note also the savings in s. 6 (6), *ante*, and s. 20 (2), *post*.

SELL
This Act applies to conditional sale agreements and hire-purchase agreements in accordance with s. 34 (3), *post*.

REPRESENTS AN INCREASE WHICH IS FORBIDDEN BY THE FOREGOING PROVISIONS
I.e., by s. 7 (2) or (3) (*a*) or (*b*) or s. 8 (2), *ante*; and note sub-s. (3) of this section. As to whether prices charged or charges made represent an increase, see s. 10, *ante*.

FINE
In the case of a body corporate there is no limit to the amount of the fine that may be imposed on indictment; but see 25 Edw. 1 (Magna Carta) (1297), c. 14 (4 Halsbury's Statutes (2nd Edn.) 24), and the Bill of Rights (1688) (Sess. 2 c. 2), s. 1 (4 Halsbury's Statutes (2nd Edn.) 152).

DEFINITIONS
For " business ", " goods ", " price " and " public notice ", see s. 34 (1), *post*.

Company distributions

12. Notice of increase in company distributions.—(1) With a view to obtaining information regarding increases in company distributions which may assist the Secretary of State and other Ministers to determine whether any question concerning any company or companies should be referred to the Board under section 2 of this Act, or whether any instruction or requirement should be given to or imposed on the Board under section 3 of this Act, the Secretary of State may by order apply this section to any companies.

(2) An order under subsection (1) above may frame a description of companies to which this section applies in any way, and in particular—

(*a*) may make distinctions by reference to the nature or scale of the trade or business carried on by any company, or the locality in which it is carried on, and

(*b*) may include or exclude named companies.

(3) Any increase in the distributions made by a company to which this section applies in any financial year shall be ascertained by reference to an earlier financial year fixed by rules prescribed by an order under this section as that company's basis financial year, and those rules—

(*a*) may prescribe different basis financial years for successive financial years of the same company, and

(*b*) may make different provision for different descriptions of companies to which this section applies, and (*c*) may fix a basis financial year which falls wholly or partly before the time when this section begins to apply to the company.

(4) If the amount of the distributions to be made by a company to which this section applies for any financial year beginning at a time when this section applies to the company, with any adjustment required by subsection (7) below, will exceed the amount of the distributions made by the company for its basis financial year, the company shall, not later than the end of a period of seven days beginning with the day on which the relevant decision regarding its distributions is taken, duly give notice to the appropriate Minister giving particulars of the amounts of the distributions made or to be made in the respective financial years, and specifying the amount of the excess.

(5) If at any time the decision on which a notice given by the company under subsection (4) above is based is set aside or varied or revoked, or there is a decision to make a distribution not taken into account in the notice, or any assumption required to be made under this section in giving the notice proves to be wrong, the company shall not later than seven days after that time give a notice to the appropriate Minister giving the particulars required to correct the earlier notice.

(6) If a company fails to comply with subsection (4) or subsection (5) above it shall be liable on summary conviction to a fine not exceeding fifty pounds.

(7) The amount of the distributions made by a company for any financial year shall for the purposes of subsection (4) above be adjusted in proportion to—

(*a*) the amount by which the issued share capital of the company at the beginning of the financial year exceeds, or is less than, its issued share capital at the beginning of the basis financial year, and

(*b*) for any difference in the length of the financial year as compared with the length of its basis financial year,

and a company's share capital at the beginning of any financial year shall be computed by taking its share capital at the beginning of its basis financial year and adjusting it—

(i) by adding the amount or value of any consideration actually received in the period between the beginning of the basis financial year and the beginning of the financial year to be compared with it for the issue of share capital or on the payment up of issued share capital, and

(ii) by deducting the amount or value of any money or other assets paid or transferred by the company during the said period for the repayment of any share capital, and the amount of the company's share capital at the beginning of the basis financial year shall be what is then the amount of the company's paid-up share capital and of any share premium account (or other comparable account by whatever name called).

(8) In this section " the relevant decision " means—

(a) where only one distribution is made by the company in the financial year, the decision to make that distribution,

(b) in any other case, any decision the implementation of which will bring the distributions made or to be made by the company for the financial year, with any adjustment required by subsection (7) above, into excess of the amount of the distributions made by the company for its basis financial year,

and " decision " means the effective decision, whether it be a declaration of dividend by the company in general meeting, or a decision of the directors, or any other decision, except that where the directors decide to recommend a dividend to be declared by the company in general meeting that decision, and not the declaration of the dividend in general meeting, shall be the decision for the purposes of this section.

(9) In applying subsection (8)(b) above, and in giving the notice required by subsection (4) above,—

(a) it shall be assumed that any preference dividend falling due after the taking of the decision in question, and any interest on securities of the company falling due after that time, will in fact be paid, and

(b) any reasonable assumption may be made as to the length of the current financial year,

but the notice under subsection (4) above shall, if it is based on the assumption of a current financial year of a length greater or less than twelve months, state that the assumption has been made and the length assumed.

(10) In this section—

" company " means any body corporate resident in the United Kingdom,

" director " includes any person occupying the position of director by whatever name called,

" distribution " has the same meaning as in Part I of Schedule 11 to the Finance Act 1965, and if a distribution is not expressed to be made for any financial year of the company it shall be regarded as made for the year in which it is payable,

" financial year " means, in relation to a company, the period in respect of which any profit and loss account of the company

[18]

laid before it in general meeting is made up, whether that period is a year or not, and " basis financial year " has the meaning given by subsection (3) above,

" preference dividend " means a dividend at a rate per cent. of the nominal value of the shares in respect of which it is paid which is fixed, or fluctuates only with the standard rate of income tax,

" share " includes stock and " share capital " shall be construed accordingly.

BRINGING OF THIS PART INTO FORCE
See s. 6, *ante*.

DULY GIVE NOTICE TO THE APPROPRIATE MINISTER
The giving of notice is to be governed by regulations made under s. 21, *post*.

SUB-S. (6): IF A COMPANY FAILS ETC.
General provisions as to offences under this Part are contained in s. 22, *post*; note also the savings in s. 6 (6), *ante*, and s. 20 (2), *post*.

SUB-S. (7): SHARE PREMIUM ACCOUNT
By the Companies Act 1948, s. 56 (3 Halsbury's Statutes (2nd Edn.) 508), where a company issues shares at a premium, a sum equal to the aggregate amount or value of the premiums is to be transferred to such an account.

STANDARD RATE OF INCOME TAX
As to the charge of income tax at the standard rate, see the Income Tax Act 1952, s. 2 (31 Halsbury's Statutes (2nd Edn.) 18).

DEFINITIONS
For " the Board ", see s. 1 (1), *ante*; for " appropriate Minister " and " Minister ", see s. 34 (1), *post*. Note also the provisions of sub-ss. (8) and (10) of this section.

FINANCE ACT 1965, SCH. 11
See 45 Halsbury's Statutes (2nd Edn.) 693. " Distribution " is defined in Part I (paras. 1–8) of this Schedule, as amended by the Finance Act 1966, s. 27, Sch. 5, para. 13, as follows:

Matters to be treated as distributions

1.—(1) in relation to any company " distribution " means—

(a) any dividend paid by the company, including a capital dividend;

(b) any other distribution out of assets of the company (whether in cash or otherwise) in respect of shares in the company, except so much of the distribution, if any, as represents a repayment of capital on the shares or is, when it is made, equal in amount or value to any new consideration given for the distribution;

(c) any redeemable share capital or [any] security issued by the company in respect of shares in the company otherwise than wholly for new consideration, or such part of any redeemable share capital or [any] security so issued as is not properly referable to new consideration;

(d) any interest or other distribution out of assets of the company in respect of securities of the company (except so much, if any, of any such distribution as represents the principal thereby secured), where the securities are either—

(i) securities issued as mentioned in paragraph (c) above; or

(ii) securities convertible directly or indirectly into shares in the company and not securities quoted on a recognised stock exchange nor issued on terms which are reasonably comparable with the terms of issue of securities so quoted; or

(iii) securities under which the consideration given by the company for the use of the principal secured is to any extent dependent on the results of the company's business or any part of it, or under which the consideration so given represents more than a reasonable commercial return for the use of that principal; or

(iv) securities [issued by the company and held by a company not resident] in the United Kingdom, where the former is a subsidiary of the latter or both are subsidiaries of a third company ("subsidiary" having the meaning assigned to it by section 42 (1) of the Finance Act 1938);

[(v) securities which are connected with shares in the company, where "connected with" means that in consequence of the nature of the rights attaching to the securities or shares, and in particular of any terms or conditions attaching to the right to transfer the shares or securities, it is necessary or advantageous for a person who has, or disposes of or acquires, any of the securities also to have, or to dispose of or to acquire, a proportionate holding of the shares];

(e) any such amount as is required to be treated as a distribution by sub-paragraph (2) or (3) below.

(2) Where on a transfer of assets or liabiliites by a company to its members or to a company by its members, the amount or value of the benefit received by the member (taken according to its market value) exceeds the amount or value (so taken) of any new consideration given by him, the company shall be treated as making a distribution to him of an amount equal to the difference.

(3) Where a company—

(a) repays any share capital, or has done so at any time after 6th April, 1965; and

(b) at or after the time of that repayment (but not before the year 1966–67) issues as paid up otherwise than by the receipt of new consideration any share capital, not being redeemable share capital;

the amount so paid up shall be treated as a distribution made in respect of the shares on which it is paid up, except in so far as that amount exceeds the amount or aggregate amount of share capital so repaid less any amounts previously so paid up and treated by virtue of this sub-paragraph as distributions.

Matters to be treated or not treated as repayments of share capital

2.—(1) Where—

(a) a company issues any share capital as paid up otherwise than by the receipt of new consideration, or has done so after 6th April 1965; and

(b) any amount so paid up does not fall to be treated as a distribution;

then for the purposes of paragraph 1 above distributions afterwards made by the company in respect of shares representing that share capital shall not be treated as repayments of share capital, except to the extent to which those distributions, together with any relevant distributions previously so made, exceed the amounts so paid up (then or previously) on such shares after that date and not falling to be treated as distributions.

(2) In sub-paragraph (1) above "relevant distribution" means so much of any distribution made in respect of shares representing the relevant share capital as apart from that sub-paragraph would be treated as a repayment of share capital, but by virtue of that sub-paragraph cannot be so treated.

(3) For the purposes of this paragraph all shares of the same class shall be treated as representing the same share capital, and where shares are issued in respect of other shares, or are directly or indirectly converted into or exchanged for other shares, all such shares shall be treated as representing the same share capital.

3.—(1) Where share capital is issued at a premium representing new consideration, the amount of the premium is to be treated as forming part of that share capital for the purpose of determining under this Part of this Schedule whether any distribution made in respect of shares representing the share capital is to be treated as a repayment of share capital:

Provided that this sub-paragraph shall not have effect in relation to any part of the premium after that part has been applied in paying up share capital.

(2) Subject to sub-paragraph (1) above, premiums paid on redemption of share capital are not to be treated as repayments of capital.

" New consideration "

4. In this Part of this Schedule " new consideration " means consideration not provided directly or indirectly out of the assets of the company, and in particular does not include amounts retained by the company by way of capitalising a distribution:

Provided that where share capital has been issued at a premium representing new consideration, any part of that premium afterwards applied in paying up share capital shall be treated as new consideration also for that share capital, except in so far as the premium has been taken into account under paragraph 3 above so as to enable a distribution to be treated as a repayment of share capital.

5. A distribution shall be treated under this Schedule as made, or consideration as provided, out of assets of a company if the cost falls on the company.

Expressions relating to shares or securities

6.—(1) In this Part of this Schedule " share " includes stock, and any other interest of a member in a company.

(2) References in this Part of this Schedule to issuing share capital as paid up apply also to the paying up of any issued share capital.

7.—(1) For purposes of this Part of this Schedule " security " includes securities not creating or evidencing a charge on assets, and interest paid by a company on money advanced without the issue of a security for the advance, or other consideration given by a company for the use of money so advanced, shall be treated as if paid or given in respect of a security issued for the advance by the company.

(2) Where securities are issued at a price less than the amount repayable on them, and are not quoted on a recognised stock exchange, the principal secured shall not be taken for the purposes of this Part of this Schedule to exceed the issue price, unless the securities are issued on terms reasonably comparable with the terms of issue of securities so quoted.

8.—(1) For purposes of this Part of this Schedule a thing is to be regarded as done in respect of a share if it is done to a person as being the holder of the share, or as having at a particular time been the holder, or is done in pursuance of a right granted or offer made in respect of a share; and anything done in respect of shares by reference to share holdings at a particular time is to be regarded as done to the then holders of the shares or the personal representatives of any share holder then dead.

(2) Sub-paragraph (1) above shall apply in relation to securities as it applies in relation to shares.

By the Finance Act 1966, s. 27, Sch. 5, para. 13 (3), para. 1 (1) (*d*) (i) of Sch. 11 to the Act of 1965 does not apply in relation to securities issued before 6th April 1965, and by para. 14 of the said Sch. 5 repayment of certain preference shares is excluded from para. 1 (3) of the said Sch. 11.

ORDERS UNDER THIS SECTION

No order had been made under sub-s. (1) up to 15th August 1966.

Terms and conditions of employment

13. Notice of pay claims and other claims.—(1) The Secretary of State may by order apply this section to any pay claims or other claims relating to terms and conditions of employment made on behalf of employees.

(2) Notice of a claim to which this section applies shall be duly given to the appropriate Minister within a period of seven days beginning with the day on which the claim is presented to the employers or employers' organisation concerned.

(3) The notice may be given—

(*a*) by the trade union or other person by whom the claim is presented, or by any trade union or trade union organisation acting on behalf of that person, or

(*b*) by the person or any of the persons to whom the claim is presented, or by any employers' organisation representing the interests of employers to whom the claim is presented.

(4) The responsibility for ensuring that notice of the claim is given in accordance with subsection (2) above shall lie both on the person by whom the claim is presented (or the trade union or trade union

organisation substituted for that person under the following provisions of this section) and on the employers or employers' organisation to whom the claim is presented, and if there is a failure to comply with subsection (2) above all of those persons shall be liable on summary conviction to a fine not exceeding fifty pounds.

(5) If a trade union or trade union organisation by notice to the Secretary of State accepts responsibility for persons specified in the notice subsection (4) above shall apply while the notice has effect as if the trade union or trade union organisation giving the notice were substituted in subsection (4) above for the persons specified in the notice.

A notice under this subsection shall take effect on notification by the Secretary of State in the Gazette of his approval given on being satisfied that the persons for whom the trade union or trade union organisation accept responsibility concur, and shall have effect subject to any varying or revoking notice taking effect in accordance with this subsection.

(6) An order under subsection (1) above may frame the descriptions of claims to which this section applies in any way, and in particular—

(*a*) may apply this section in relation to employees in specified kinds of work, or in specified localities, or working in specified undertakings or for specified employers,

(*b*) in applying it in relation to employees working in specified undertakings or for specified employers, may make distinctions as regards those undertakings and persons by reference to the regions or localities where the undertakers or employers carry on business, or the number of employees working in the undertakings or for the employers, or by reference to any other different circumstances, and may be made so as to apply to named undertakings or persons,

(*c*) may make distinctions by reference to the subject matter of the claims, including in particular distinctions between claims relating to pay and claims relating to other terms and conditions of employment, or by reference to the amount of any increase in pay which is claimed.

(7) This section shall not apply in relation to a claim presented before the coming into force of the order bringing within this section claims of the description embracing that claim.

BRINGING OF THIS PART INTO FORCE
See s. 6, *ante.*

NOTICE...DULY GIVEN TO THE APPROPRIATE MINISTER
The giving of notices is to be governed by regulations made under s. 21, *post.*

SEVEN DAYS BEGINNING WITH THE DAY, ETC.
Cf. the note " Thirty days beginning with the date, etc." to s. 7, *ante.*

IF THERE IS A FAILURE TO COMPLY, ETC.
General provisions as to offences under this Part are contained in s. 22, *post*; note also the savings in s. 6 (6), *ante*, and s. 20 (2), *post*.

EMPLOYMENT UNDER THE CROWN
See s. 18, *post*.

DEFINITIONS
For " appropriate Minister " and " employee ", see s. 34 (1), *post*; for " trade union ", see (by virtue of s. 34 (1), *post*) the Trade Union Act 1913, s. 2 (1) (25 Halsbury's Statutes (2nd Edn.) 1271); for " Gazette ", see s. 34 (4), *post*.

ORDERS UNDER THIS SECTION
No order has been made under sub-s. (1) up to 15th August 1966.
For general provisions as to orders made under this Part of the Act, see see s. 20, *post*, and s. 6 (4), *ante*.

14. Notice of awards and settlements.—(1) The Secretary of State may by order apply this section to awards and settlements relating to terms or conditions of employment.

(2) Within seven days of the making of an award or settlement to which this section applies the employers affected by the award or settlement shall duly give notice, with particulars of the award or settlement, to the appropriate Minister; and an employer failing to comply with this subsection shall be liable on summary conviction to a fine not exceeding fifty pounds.

(3) The notice to be given as required by subsection (2) above may be so given by a trade union or other person representing the employees affected by the award or settlement, or by a trade union organisation acting on behalf of those employees, and, if so given within the period specified in that subsection, shall absolve the employers affected by the award or settlement from the responsibility imposed by that subsection; and notices to be given by any employers under subsection (2) above may be so given on their behalf by any one of them, or by any employers' organisation representing their interests.

(4) The receipt by the appropriate Minister of a notice duly given under subsection (2) or subsection (3) above shall be notified in the Gazette.

(5) An award or settlement to which this section applies shall not be implemented unless the notice required by this section has been duly given to the appropriate Minister.

(6) When the notice required by this section has been duly given to the appropriate Minister—

(*a*) the award or settlement shall not be implemented until after the expiration of a period of thirty days beginning with the date on which the notice is so given, except that if at any earlier time the said Minister publishes in the Gazette a notice stating that it has been decided not to refer the award or settlement to the Board, this paragraph shall apply only until that earlier time,

(b) if under section 2(1) or 2(3) of this Act the award or settlement is referred to the Board by a reference published in the Gazette within the said period of thirty days, the award or settlement shall not without the written consent of the Minister or Ministers who referred it be implemented until the date of publication of the Board's report on the reference.

Any written consent given under paragraph (b) above shall be notified in the Gazette.

(7) An order under subsection (1) above may frame the descriptions of awards and settlements to which this section applies in any way, and in particular may contain provisions corresponding to those authorised, in framing descriptions of claims, by paragraphs (a), (b) and (c) of section 13(6) of this Act.

(8) This section shall not apply in relation to an award or settlement made before the coming into force of the order bringing within this section awards or settlements of the description embracing that award or settlement.

BRINGING OF THIS PART INTO FORCE
See s. 6, *ante.*

WITHIN SEVEN DAYS
Cf. the note " Within three months " to s. 5, *ante.*

DULY GIVE NOTICE ... TO THE APPROPRIATE MINISTER
The giving of notices is to be governed by regulations made under s. 21, *post.*

EMPLOYER FAILING TO COMPLY, ETC.
General provisions as to offences under this Part are contained in s. 22, *post*; note also the savings in s. 6 (6), *ante*, and s. 20 (2), *post.*

AWARD OR SETTLEMENT ... SHALL NOT BE IMPLEMENTED
As to offences and the punishment thereof, see s. 16, *post.*

THIRTY DAYS BEGINNING WITH THE DATE, ETC.
Cf. the note to s. 7, *ante.*

PUBLISHED IN THE GAZETTE WITHIN THE SAID PERIOD OF THIRTY DAYS
As to the date of publication in the Gazette, see s. 34 (4), *post.*

DATE OF PUBLICATION OF THE BOARD'S REPORT
As to this date, see s. 5 (1), *ante.* By s. 19 (1), *post,* if the report of the Board on a question referred to them under s. 2 (1), *ante,* is not published in accordance with the said s. 5 (1) by a date within three months from the publication of the reference sub-s. (6) (b) of this section is to apply as if the report had been so published on the last day of that period; see also s. 19 (2), *post,* as to the application of sub-s. (6) (b) in relation to interim or partial reports.

EMPLOYMENT UNDER THE CROWN
See s. 18, *post.*

DEFINITIONS
For " the Board ", see s. 1 (1), *ante*; for " appropriate Minister ", " awards and settlements ", " employee " and " Minister ", see s. 34 (1), *post*; for " trade union ", see (by virtue of s. 34 (1), *post*) the Trade Union Act 1913, s. 2 (1) (25 Halsbury's Statutes (2nd Edn.) 1271); for " Gazette ", see s. 34 (4), *post*.

ORDERS UNDER THIS SECTION
No order had been made under sub-s. (1) up to 15th August 1966.
For general provisions as to orders made under this Part of the Act, see s. 20, *post*, and s. 6 (4), *ante*.

15. Standstill for other awards and settlements.—(1) If under section 2(1) or 2(3) of this Act any award or settlement is referred to the Board, the Secretary of State, or the Secretary of State acting jointly with any other Minister, may by notice published in the issue of the Gazette in which the text of the reference is published, direct that this section shall apply to the award or settlement.

(2) An award or settlement to which this section applies shall not be implemented until the date of publication of the Board's report on the reference except that if at any earlier time the direction under sub-section (1) above is revoked in whole or in part by notice published in the Gazette by the Minister or Ministers who gave the direction this sub-section shall apply, or as the case may be shall apply in relation to the matters affected by the partial revocation, only until that earlier time.

(3) This section shall not apply in relation to an employer who first implements the award or settlement before the publication in the Gazette of the direction under subsection (1) above.

BRINGING OF THIS PART INTO FORCE
See s. 6, *ante*.

TEXT OF THE REFERENCE IS PUBLISHED
I.e., under s. 2 (4), *ante*.

AWARD OR SETTLEMENT . . . SHALL NOT BE IMPLEMENTED
As to offences and the punishment thereof, see s. 16, *post*.

DATE OF PUBLICATION OF THE BOARD'S REPORT
As to this date, see s. 5 (1), *ante*. By virtue of s. 19 (1), *post*, if the report of the Board on a question referred to them under s. 2 (1), *ante*, is not published in accordance with the said s. 5 (1) by a date within three months from the publication of the reference, this section is to apply as if the report had been so published on the last day of that period; see also s. 19 (2), *post*, as to the application of this section in relation to interim or partial reports.

EMPLOYMENT UNDER THE CROWN
See s. 18, *post*.

DEFINITIONS
For " the Board ", see s. 1 (1), *ante*; for " awards and settlements " and " Minister ", see s. 34 (1), *post*; for " Gazette ", see s. 34 (4), *post*.

16. Terms and conditions of employment: enforcement.—(1) It shall be an offence for an employer to implement an award or settlement in respect of employment at a time when the implementation of the award or settlement is forbidden under the foregoing provisions of this Part of this Act.

[*25*]

(2) Subsection (1) above shall not make it unlawful for an employer, at a time when the implementation of an award or settlement is not forbidden by the foregoing provisions of this Part of this Act, to pay any sum in respect of remuneration for employment at an earlier time.

(3) A person guilty of an offence under subsection (1) of this section shall be liable—

(a) on summary conviction to a fine not exceeding one hundred pounds, and

(b) on conviction on indictment to a fine which, if the offender is not a body corporate, shall not exceed five hundred pounds.

(4) If any trade union or other person takes, or threatens to take, any action, and in particular any action by way of taking part, or persuading others to take part, in a strike, with a view to compel, induce or influence any employer to implement an award or settlement in respect of employment at a time when the implementation of that award or settlement is forbidden under the foregoing provisions of this Part of this Act, he shall be liable—

(a) on summary conviction to a fine not exceeding one hundred pounds, and

(b) on conviction on indictment to a fine which, if the offender is not a body corporate, shall not exceed five hundred pounds.

(5) This section shall not give rise to any criminal or tortious liability for conspiracy or any other liability in tort.

(6) The last foregoing subsection shall not apply in Scotland but where any act is prohibited by this section, the fact that it is so prohibited shall be treated as irrelevant for the purposes of any civil proceedings in Scotland.

Sub-sections (4)–(6) of this section are applied by s. 28 (4), (5) in Part IV, *post* (see also s. 25 (9), *post*).

BRINGING OF THIS PART INTO FORCE
See s. 6, *ante*.

IT SHALL BE AN OFFENCE
General provisions as to offences under this Part are contained in s. 22, *post*; note also the savings in s. 6 (6), *ante*, and s. 20 (2), *post*.

IMPLEMENTATION OF THE AWARD OR SETTLEMENT IS FORBIDDEN UNDER THE FOREGOING PROVISIONS
I.e., under s. 14 (5) or (6) (a) or (b) or 15 (2), *ante*.

FINE
See the note to s. 11, *ante*.

EMPLOYMENT UNDER THE CROWN
See s. 8, *post*.

DEFINITIONS
For "awards and settlements", see s. 34 (1), *post*; for "trade union", see (by virtue of s. 34 (1), *post*) the Trade Union Act 1913, s. 2 (1) (25 Halsbury's Statutes (2nd Edn.) 1271).

17. Meaning of " trade dispute ".—The expression " trade dispute " as defined by section 5(3) of the Trade Disputes Act 1906 shall include any dispute between employers and workmen, or between workmen and workmen, which is connected with the restrictions imposed by this Part of this Act, and " dispute " shall include any difference of opinion as to the manner in which account is to be taken of the provisions of this Part of this Act.

This section is applied by s. 28 (6) in Part IV, *post* (see also s. 25 (9), *post*).

GENERAL NOTE
Under certain enactments the consequences which would normally follow upon certain acts may be avoided when those acts are done in contemplation or furtherance of a trade dispute. The enactments particularly concerned are the Trade Disputes Act 1906, s. 2 (25 Halsbury's Statutes (2nd Edn.) 1267) (peaceful picketing); s. 3 of that Act (25 Halsbury's Statutes (2nd Edn.) 1268) (removal of liability for interfering with another person's business, etc.); the Trade Disputes Act 1965, s. 1 (45 Halsbury's Statutes (2nd Edn.) 1755) (certain acts not actionable in tort); and the Conspiracy, and Protection of Property Act 1875, s. 3 (5 Halsbury's Statutes (2nd Edn.) 886) (amendment of law as to conspiracy in trade disputes). The protection thus afforded is now extended to cover disputes between employers and workmen, or between workmen and workmen, which arise out of the restrictions imposed by this Part of this Act or (by virtue of s. 28 (6), *post*) Part IV hereof.

BRINGING OF THIS PART INTO FORCE
See s. 6, *ante*.

WORKMEN
This expression is defined by the Trade Disputes Act 1906, s. 5 (3) (25 Halsbury's Statutes (2nd Edn.) 1269) to mean all persons employed in trade or industry, whether or not in the employment of the employer with whom a trade dispute arises.

EMPLOYMENT UNDER THE CROWN
See s. 18, *infra*.

TRADE DISPUTES ACT 1906, s. 5 (3)
See 25 Halsbury's Statutes (2nd Edn.) 1269. By that subsection the definition of " trade dispute " therein applies not only for the purposes of the Act of 1906 but also for the purposes of the Conspiracy, and Protection of Property Act 1875 (5 Halsbury's Statutes (2nd Edn.) 885; and by the Trade Disputes Act 1965, s. 1 (1) (45 Halsbury's Statutes (2nd Edn.) 1755), this definition applies as well for the purposes of the Act of 1965. As to these enactments, see also the General Note, *supra*.

18. Employment under the Crown.—(1) Although this Part of this Act does not bind the Crown a notice may be given under section 15 of this Act so as, without imposing any obligation on the Crown as an employer or otherwise, to apply to persons employed by or under the Crown, and subsections (4), (5) and (6) of section 16, and section 17, of this Act shall apply accordingly.

(2) Sections 13 and 14 of this Act shall not apply to or in relation to any person as an employee where, because the employer is the Crown,

those sections do not impose any obligation on that person's employer.

(3) For the purposes of this Act employment by any such body as is specified in Schedule 3 to the Redundancy Payments Act 1965 (national health service employers) shall (if it would not otherwise be so regarded) be regarded as employment by or under the Crown.

(4) In the application of this section to Northern Ireland references to the Crown include references to the Crown in right of the Government of Northern Ireland.

Sub-sections (3) and (4) of this section are applied by s. 28 (5) in Part IV, *post* (see also s. 25 (9), *post*).

BRINGING OF THIS PART INTO FORCE
See s. 6, *ante*.

DOES NOT BIND THE CROWN
This section must be read in the light of the rule (as to which, see 36 Halsbury's Laws (3rd Edn.) 430 *et seq*.) that the Crown is not bound by the provisions of a statute unless the contrary is expressly stated or necessarily implied.

EMPLOYEE
For meaning, see s. 34 (1), *post*.

REDUNDANCY PAYMENTS ACT 1965, SCH. 3
See 45 Halsbury's Statutes (2nd Edn.) 341.

Supplemental

19. Reports on references to which Part II applies.—(1) If the report of the Board on a question referred to the Board under section 2(1) of this Act (whether or not varied under section 2(3) of this Act) is not published in accordance with section 5(1) of this Act by a date within three months from the publication of the reference, the following provisions of this Act—

section 7(3)(*b*),
section 8,
section 14(6)(*b*),
section 15,

shall apply as if the report had been so published on the last day of that period.

(2) The said provisions of this Act shall apply in relation to a report notwithstanding that it is expressed to be an interim report or to deal with part only of the question referred to the Board.

BRINGING OF THIS PART INTO FORCE
See s. 6, *ante*.

THE BOARD
I.e., the National Board for Prices and Incomes; see s. 1 (1), *ante*.

WITHIN THREE MONTHS
See the note to s. 5, *ante*. The Board's report is required to be published within three months by virtue of s. 5 (3), *ante*, unless the period is extended under s. 5 (4), *ante*. It would appear, however, that for the purposes of the present section no such extension affects the limit of three months mentioned in sub-s. (1) hereof.

20. Orders made by Secretary of State.—(1) An order made by the Secretary of State under this Part of this Act—

(*a*) may be varied or revoked by a subsequent order so made,

(*b*) shall be contained in a statutory instrument subject to annulment in pursuance of a resolution of either House of Parliament.

(2) The variation or revocation of an order made under this section shall not affect liability for any offence committed before the variation or revocation takes effect.

BRINGING OF THIS PART INTO FORCE
See s. 6, *ante*.

STATUTORY INSTRUMENT SUBJECT TO ANNULMENT
See the note to s. 1, *ante*.

ORDER MADE UNDER THIS SECTION
It would appear that these words in sub-s. (2) should read " order made under this Part of this Act ".

21. Regulations about notices to Ministers.—The Secretary of State may by regulations in a statutory instrument subject to annulment in pursuance of a resolution of either House of Parliament—

(*a*) prescribe the form of any notice to be given to a Minister under this Part of this Act, the manner in which any such notice is to be given and the evidence which is to be sufficient evidence of its having been given,

(*b*) prescribe the particulars to be contained in any such notice,

(*c*) authorise a notice to be given by any persons to be given on their behalf by such organisation, body or person as may be prescribed by the regulations, and

(*d*) define " the appropriate Minister " for the purposes of any such notice,

and regulations under this section may make different provision for different cases.

This section is applied by s. 25 (6), in Part IV, *post* (see also s. 25 (9), *post*).

BRINGING OF THIS PART INTO FORCE
See s. 6, *ante*.

For meaning, see s. 34 (1), *post*.

REGULATIONS UNDER THIS SECTION
No regulations had been made under this section up to 15th August 1966.

22. Offences under Part II.—(1) Proceedings for an offence under this Part of this Act shall not be instituted in England or Wales except by or with the consent of the Attorney General, and shall not be instituted in Northern Ireland except by or with the consent of the Attorney General for Northern Ireland.

(2) Where an offence is alleged to have been committed under this Part of this Act by a trade union, trade union organisation, or employers' organisation, being an unincorporated body—

(a) proceedings for the offence shall be brought in the name of that body (and not in that of any of its members),

(b) for the purpose of any such proceedings any rules of court relating to the service of documents shall have effect as if that body were a corporation, and

(c) any fine imposed on conviction shall be payable out of the funds of that body.

(3) Where an offence mentioned in subsection (2) above is an offence punishable on conviction on indictment, section 33 of the Criminal Justice Act 1925, Schedule 2 to the Magistrates' Courts Act 1952, section 18 of the Criminal Justice Act (Northern Ireland) 1945 and Schedule 5 to the Magistrates' Courts Act (Northern Ireland) 1964 (procedure on charge of offence against a corporation) shall have effect as if the said body were a corporation.

(4) In relation to any proceedings on indictment in Scotland for an offence alleged to have been committed under this Part of this Act by a body such as is mentioned in subsection (2) above, section 40 of the Criminal Justice (Scotland) Act 1949 (proceedings on indictment against bodies corporate) shall have effect as if the said body were a body corporate.

(5) Where an offence under this Part of this Act committed by a body corporate is proved to have been committed with the consent or connivance of, or to be attributable to any neglect on the part of, any director, manager, secretary or other similar officer of the body corporate or any person who was purporting to act in any such capacity, he as well as the body corporate shall be guilty of that offence and shall be liable to be proceeded against and punished accordingly.

In this subsection "director", in relation to a body corporate established by or under any enactment (including an enactment of the

[*30*]

Parliament of Northern Ireland) for the purpose of carrying on under national ownership any industry or undertaking or part of an industry or undertaking, being a body corporate whose affairs are managed by its members, means a member of that body corporate.

This section is applied by s. 25 (6) in Part IV, *post* (see also s. 25 (9), *post*), and sub-ss. (2), (3) and (5) thereof are applied by s. 1 (7), *ante*, and Sch. 1, para. 14 (5), *post*.

BRINGING OF THIS PART INTO FORCE
See s. 6, *ante*.

ATTORNEY GENERAL
In certain cases the Solicitor General may discharge the functions of the Attorney General; see the Law Officers Act 1944, s. 1 (4 Halsbury's Statutes (2nd Edn.) 540). See also, as to evidence of the consent of the Attorney General, the Criminal Justice Act 1925, s. 34 (14 Halsbury's Statutes (2nd Edn.) 956).

ATTORNEY GENERAL FOR NORTHERN IRELAND
See, as to the case where a deputy is appointed to act as Attorney General for Northern Ireland, the Law Officers Act 1944, s. 3 (4 Halsbury's Statutes (2nd Edn.) 541); and see, as to evidence of the consent of the Attorney General for Northern Ireland or his deputy, the Criminal Justice Act (Northern Ireland) 1945 (N.I.), s. 19.

TRADE UNION
For meaning, see (by virtue of s. 34 (1), *post*) the Trade Union Act 1913, s. 2 (1) (25 Halsbury's Statutes (2nd Edn.) 1271).

RULES OF COURT RELATING TO THE SERVICE OF DOCUMENTS
See, *e.g.*, the Magistrates' Courts Rules 1952, S.I. 1952 No. 2190, r. 76 (13 Halsbury's Statutory Instruments, title Magistrates (Part 1)). The expression " rules of court " is defined by the Interpretation Act 1889, s. 14 (24 Halsbury's Statutes (2nd Edn.) 217).

OFFENCE . . . COMMITTED BY A BODY CORPORATE
Except where the penalty is inappropriate or where, by the nature of the offence, it must be committed by an individual, a corporation may be convicted for the criminal acts of its agent or servant acting within the scope of his authority, and the knowledge or intention of the servant may be imputed to the corporation; see *Director of Public Prosecutions* v. *Kent and Sussex Contractors, Ltd.*, [1944] 1 All E.R. 119; [1944] K.B. 146, and *R.* v. *I.C.R. Haulage, Ltd.*, [1944] 1 All E.R. 641; [1944] K.B. 551, C.C.A.
For the general law relating to corporations, see 9 Halsbury's Laws (3rd Edn.) 3 *et seq.*

CONSENT
There is authority for saying that this presupposes knowledge; see *Re Caughey, Ex parte Ford* (1876), 1 Ch.D. 521, C.A., at p. 528, *per* Jessel, M.R., and *Lamb* v. *Wright & Co.*, [1924] 1 K.B. 857; [1924] All E.R. Rep. 220, at p. 864 and p. 223, respectively. It is thought, however, that actual knowledge is not necessary; cf. *Knox* v. *Boyd*, 1941 S.C. (J.) 82, at p. 86, and *Taylor's Central Garages (Exeter), Ltd.* v. *Roper* (1951), 115 J.P. 445, at pp. 449, 450, *per* Devlin, J.; and see also, in particular, *Mallon* v. *Allon*, [1963] 3 All E.R. 843; [1964] 1 Q.B. 385, at p. 847 and p. 394, respectively.

CONNIVANCE
This, it has been said, implies knowledge and acquiescence and as a legal doctrine has its source and its limits in the principle *volenti non fit injuria*; see *Boulting* v. *Boulting* (1864), 3 Sw. & Tr. 329, at p. 335, *per* Sir James Wilde.

Yet, here again, it seems that actual knowledge is not necessary and suspicion is enough, although mere negligence or inattention is not; see *Rogers* v. *Rogers* (1830), 3 Hag. Ecc. 57 (but note the express reference in sub-s. (4) to neglect). See also, in particular, *Douglas* v. *Douglas*, [1950] 2 All E.R. 748; [1951] P. 85, C.A.; *Godfrey* v. *Godfrey*, [1964] 3 All E.R. 154; [1965] A.C. 444, H.L.; and *Rumbelow* v. *Rumbelow and Hadden*, [1965] 2 All E.R. 767, C.A.

NEGLECT
This term, in the words of Simonds, J. (as he then was), in *Re Hughes, Rea* v. *Black*, [1943] 2 All E.R. 269; [1943] Ch. 296, at p. 271 and p. 298, respectively, " in its legal connotation implies failure to perform a duty which the person knows or ought to know ". This, it is thought, is also the meaning that the expression has in the present context.

ANY PERSON WHO WAS PURPORTING TO ACT, ETC.
These words are inserted in view of the decision in *Dean* v. *Hiesler*, [1942] 2 All E.R. 340, that a director who had not been validly appointed was not liable for an offence committed by the company.

CRIMINAL JUSTICE ACT 1925, s. 33
See 14 Halsbury's Statutes (2nd Edn.) 954. Sub-sections (1), (2) and (5) of that section were repealed by the Magistrates' Courts Act 1952, s. 132, Sch. 6 (32 Halsbury's Statutes (2nd Edn.) 523, 524).

MAGISTRATES' COURTS ACT 1952, SCH. 2
See 32 Halsbury's Statutes (2nd Edn.) 525.

CRIMINAL JUSTICE ACT (NORTHERN IRELAND) 1945
1945 c. 15 (N.I.).

MAGISTRATES' COURTS ACT (NORTHERN IRELAND) 1964
1964 c. 21 (N.I.).

CRIMINAL JUSTICE (SCOTLAND) ACT 1949
12, 13 & 14 Geo. 6 c. 94.

PART III

MISCELLANEOUS

23. Duty of certain price-regulating bodies to have regard to consider-ations referred to in s. 4.—(1) Subject to the following subsection, any person or body having functions under any enactment in connection with the regulation of prices or charges of any of the descriptions specified in paragraph 2 of Schedule 3 to this Act shall, in the exercise of those functions, have regard, in addition to and so far as consistent with any other matters which they may be required to take into account, to the considerations set out in Schedule 2 to this Act, as for the time being added to or modified by any order of the Secretary of State under section 4(2) thereof.

(2) The foregoing subsection applies to the Air Transport Licensing Board and the Minister of Aviation in the exercise of their functions under the Civil Aviation (Licensing) Act 1960 only so far as those functions relate to charges on domestic services.

(3) The reference in subsection (2) above to charges on domestic services is a reference to all charges in respect of services between

terminal points one of which is in the United Kingdom and the other of which is in the United Kingdom, one of the Channel Islands or the Isle of Man, with the exception of charges for carriage between any such points where the carriage forms part of carriage to or from a place which is not in the United Kingdom, one of the Channel Islands or the Isle of Man, and the tariff applicable to those charges is one for the whole of the last-mentioned carriage.

AIR TRANSPORT LICENSING BOARD
    This board is established by the Civil Aviation (Licensing) Act 1960, s. 1 (1), Sch. (40 Halsbury's Statutes (2nd Edn.) 27, 41).

UNITED KINGDOM
    See the note to s. 9, *ante*.

CIVIL AVIATION (LICENSING) ACT 1960
    See 40 Halsbury's Statutes (2nd Edn.) 26.

24. Exclusion from Restrictive Trade Practices Act 1956 of approved agreements and recommendations with respect to prices.—(1) The Secretary of State and the President of the Board of Trade acting jointly may, if they consider it expedient to do so having regard to any recommendation as to prices contained in a report of the Board under this Act, approve the inclusion in any proposed agreement of any term as respects which they are satisfied that the conditions specified in subsection (2) below are fulfilled, or the making by any trade association of any recommendation as respects which they are similarly satisfied; and—

(*a*) in determining whether an agreement is one to which Part I of the Restrictive Trade Practices Act 1956 applies, no account shall be taken of any term included therein pursuant to an approval under this section (and accordingly, section 8 (9) of that Act shall have effect as if the restrictions accepted by any such term were accepted by a term of which account cannot be taken by virtue of section 7 thereof);

(*b*) section 6(7) of that Act shall not apply to any recommendation made pursuant to such an approval.

(2) The said conditions are—

(*a*) that the term or recommendation in question relates exclusively to the prices to be charged in connection with transactions of a character dealt with by the relevant recommendation of the Board, or transactions of a character substantially similar to those so dealt with; and

(*b*) that the said term or recommendation is expressed to continue in force for a period not exceeding two years from the date on which it takes effect.

[*33*]

(3) No order made by the Court before or after the passing of this Act under Part I of the Restrictive Trade Practices Act 1956 (jurisdiction as respects restrictions which are contrary to the public interest), and no undertaking given before or after the passing of this Act in proceedings under that Part, shall prevent the making of an agreement which, in consequence of an approval under this section, is not an agreement to which the said Part I applies, or prevent the making of a recommendation pursuant to an approval under this section.

(4) An approval under this section shall be given in writing, and shall identify the report containing the relevant recommendation of the Board.

(5) In this section " agreement " has the same meaning as in Part I of the said Act of 1956.

THE COURT
   " The Court " for the purposes of the Restrictive Trade Practices Act 1956, Part I (36 Halsbury's Statutes (2nd Edn.) 934) is the Restrictive Practices Court established by s. 2 of that Act (36 Halsbury's Statutes (2nd Edn.) 935).

WRITING
   See the note " Written " to s. 7, *ante*.

DEFINITIONS
   For " the Board ", see s. 1 (1), *ante*; for " price " and " trade association ", see s. 34 (1), *post*. Note as to " agreement ", sub-s. (5) of this section.

RESTRICTIVE TRADE PRACTICES ACT 1956, PART I, SS. 6 (7), 7, 8 (9)
   See 36 Halsbury's Statutes (2nd Edn.) 934, 938, 939, 941. For the meaning in Part I of that Act (which relates to the registration and judicial investigation of restrictive trading agreements) of " agreement ", see s. 6 (3) thereof; and as to the agreements to which that Part applies, see ss. 6-8 of that Act (36 Halsbury's Statutes (2nd Edn.) 937-940).

PART IV

TEMPORARY RESTRICTIONS ON PRICES AND INCOMES

25. General provisions as to operation of Part IV.—(1) At any time in the period of twelve months beginning with the date of the passing of this Act Her Majesty may by Order in Council bring the provisions of this Part of this Act into force for the remainder of the said period of twelve months.

An Order in Council made under this subsection shall cease to have effect at the expiration of a period of twenty-eight days beginning with the date on which it is made unless before the end of that period the Order has been approved by a resolution of each House of Parliament.

(2) Without prejudice to the provisions of section 37 of the Interpretation Act 1889, any power of making orders or regulations under the following provisions of this Act may be exercised before those provisions

are brought into force under subsection (1) above, but not so as to have any effect before they are so brought into force.

(3) Her Majesty may by Order in Council at any time revoke an Order in Council made under subsection (1) above.

(4) If this Part of this Act is brought into force by an Order in Council under subsection (1) above, the lapse of its provisions at the end of the period of twelve months mentioned in that subsection, or on the revocation or cessation of the Order in Council, shall not affect liability for any offence committed before the lapse of those provisions.

(5) An order made by the Secretary of State under the following provisions of this Part of this Act—

(*a*) may be varied or revoked by a subsequent order so made,

(*b*) shall be contained in a statutory instrument subject to annulment in pursuance of a resolution of either House of Parliament,

and the variation or revocation of an order in pursuance of this section shall not affect liability for any offence committed before the variation or revocation takes effect.

(6) Sections 21 and 22 of this Act shall apply as if references in those sections to Part II of this Act included references to this Part of this Act, and regulations under the said section 21 as so applied may provide for the manner in which notices may be served under this Part of this Act by the Secretary of State or any other Minister and may define " the appropriate Minister " for any of the purposes of this Part of this Act.

(7) In comparing for the purposes of this Part of this Act the amount of any price or charge, or the rate of any remuneration, with earlier prices or charges or remuneration paid before any specified date, so far as required for the purpose of giving effect to any order or direction under the following provisions of this Part of this Act—

(*a*) account shall only be taken of such earlier prices or charges or remuneration as fell within such period ending immediately before the specified date as is prescribed by the order or direction, and

(*b*) as between earlier and later prices or charges or remuneration falling within that period, account shall only be taken of the later or latest.

(8) In cases where—

(*a*) in pursuance of an order under this Part of this Act a comparison is to be made between rates of remuneration for work at different times, and

(*b*) there are normal working hours for the work, and any of the remuneration to be considered consists of or includes remuneration for work outside those normal working hours,

[*35*]

the order may prescribe the manner in which the comparison is to be made, including in particular the adjustments which are to be made where the normal working hours are shorter at the later time.

In this subsection " normal working hours " has the meaning given by paragraph 1 of Schedule 2 to the Contracts of Employment Act 1963 or, for the purposes of any order under this Part of this Act, such other meaning as may be assigned by that order.

(9) Any provision in this Part of this Act which applies a provision in Part II of this Act shall have effect at all times whether or not Part II of this Act is then in force.

TWELVE MONTHS (TWENTY-EIGHT DAYS) BEGINNING WITH THE DATE, ETC.
Cf. the note " Thirty days beginning with the date, etc." to s. 7, *ante.*

PASSING OF THIS ACT
This Act was passed (*i.e.,* received the Royal Assent) on 12th August 1966.

STATUTORY INSTRUMENT SUBJECT TO ANNULMENT
See the note to s. 1, *ante.*

INTERPRETATION ACT 1889, S. 37
See 24 Halsbury's Statutes (2nd Edn.) 228.

CONTRACTS OF EMPLOYMENT ACT 1963, SCH. 2, PARA. 1
See 43 Halsbury's Statutes (2nd Edn.) 287.

> The expression "normal working hours" is defined in that paragraph as follows:
> 1 (1) For the purposes of this Schedule the cases where there are normal working hours include cases where the employee is entitled to overtime pay when employed for more than a fixed number of hours in a week or other period, and, subject to the following subparagraph, in those cases that fixed number of hours (in this paragraph referred to as " the number of hours without overtime ") shall be the normal working hours.
> (2) If in such a case—
>> (*a*) the contract of employment fixes the number, or the minimum number, of hours of employment in the said week or other period (whether or not it also provides for the reduction of that number or minimum number of hours in certain circumstances), and
>> (*b*) that number or minimum number of hours exceeds the number of hours without overtime,
> that number or minimim number of hours (and not the number of hours without overtime) shall be the normal working hours.

ORDERS IN COUNCIL UNDER THIS SECTION
No Order in Council had been made under this section up to 15th August 1966. An Order in Council could be made on 21st September 1966 for approval by Parliament on 18th October 1966, the date on which, under present arrangements, Parliament resumes after the Summer Recess.
The powers to make Orders in Council are exercisable by statutory instrument; see the Statutory Instruments Act 1946, s. 1 (1) (24 Halsbury's Statutes (2nd Edn.) 441).

26. Restrictions on increases of prices or charges.—(1) The Secretary of State may by order apply this section to any prices for the sale of goods and to any charges for the performance of services, including charges for the application of any process to goods.

(2) Prices or charges to which this section applies for transactions effected by a person in the course of business shall not exceed by any amount the prices or charges for transactions of the same description effected by that person in the course of business before the coming into force of the order applying this section to the prices or charges unless the appropriate Minister has given his consent in writing to an excess of that amount, or of a greater amount.

(3) This section shall not apply in relation to prices paid on any sale by auction.

(4) An order under subsection (1) above may frame a description of prices or charges to which this section applies in any way, and in particular in framing a description of prices of goods of a specified class—

(a) may make distinctions by reference to the undertakings or persons selling the goods,

(b) may make distinctions by reference to the terms and conditions on which the goods are sold, the quantity sold or the undertakings or persons to whom they are sold,

(c) may make distinctions by reference to the undertakings or persons by whom the goods have been produced or dealt with, or the locality in which they have been produced,

(d) in making any of the distinctions above as regards undertakings or persons, may distinguish undertakings or persons by reference to the regions or localities where they carry on business or the scale or turnover of their business or by reference to any other circumstances, and may include or exclude named undertakings or named persons,

and comparable distinctions may be made in relation to charges for the performance of services.

(5) An order under subsection (1) above may provide for the manner in which account is to be taken of any discount allowed in any transaction and may be applied both to any price before discount is allowed and also to any price after allowance of discount.

(6) An order under this section shall contain such provisions for excluding prices and charges as appear to the Secretary of State making the order practicable and appropriate for the purpose of ensuring that this section does not impede the export trade (that is to say the provision of goods and services for persons not resident in the United Kingdom).

(7) If, by a sale of goods, or by the performance of services, effected at a time when the order under this section is in force, any person contravenes subsection (2) of this section he shall be liable—

(a) on summary conviction to a fine not exceeding one hundred pounds, and (*b*) on conviction on indictment to a fine which, if the offender is not a body corporate, shall not exceed five hundred pounds.

BRINGING OF THIS PART INTO FORCE
See s. 25, *ante*.

SALE OF GOODS
This Act applies to conditional sale agreements and hire-purchase agreements in accordance with s. 34 (3), *post*.

SHALL NOT EXCEED
The restriction imposed by sub-s. (2) must be read in the light of any provision made by virtue of s. 25 (7), *ante*. As to recovery of any excess over the lawful amount, see s. 33 (1), *post*.

WRITING
See the note " Written " to s. 7, *ante*.

UNITED KINGDOM
See the note to s. 9, *ante*.

IF . . . ANY PERSON CONTRAVENES, ETC.
The general provisions as to offences contained in s. 22, *ante*, are applied by s. 25 (6), *ante*; note also the savings in s. 25 (4), (5), *ante*.

FINE
See the note to s. 11, *ante*.

DEFINITIONS
For " appropriate Minister ", " business ", " goods " and " price ", see s. 34 (1), *post* (and see also, as to " the appropriate Minister ", s. 25 (6), *ante*).

ORDERS UNDER THIS SECTION
No order had been made under sub-s. (1) up to 15th August 1966.
For general provisions as to orders made under this Part of the Act, see s. 25 (2), (5), *ante*.

27. Restrictions on prices and charges by reference to levels at 20th July 1966.—(1) A Minister may give notice in writing to any person who was carrying on a business on 20th July 1966 which included the selling of goods or the performance of services that the Minister is considering the giving of a direction under this section as respects the prices or charges for any such goods or services.

(2) A notice under subsection (1) above shall give particulars of the direction proposed to be given, and shall specify a period, which shall be not less than fourteen days from the service of the notice, within which the said person may make representations in writing to the Minister.

(3) The Minister may, if he thinks fit, after the expiration of the period specified in the notice for the making of representations, and after considering any representations duly made, by notice served on the said person direct that this section shall apply to such prices for the sale of goods by the said person, or to such charges for the performance

of services by the said person, including charges for the application of any process to goods, as may be specified in the direction, being prices or charges for transactions effected by the said person in the course of business.

(4) Prices or charges to which this section applies shall not exceed prices or charges for transactions of the same description effected by the said person in the course of business before 20th July 1966 by any amount unless—

(*a*)   the Minister has given his consent in writing to an excess of that amount, or of a greater amount, or

(*b*)   the direction authorises an excess of that amount, or of a greater amount.

(5) A direction under this section may frame the descriptions of prices or charges to which this section applies in any way, and in particular may contain provisions corresponding to those authorised by subsections (4) and (5) of the last foregoing section.

(6) This section shall not apply in relation to prices paid on any sale by auction.

(7) Subsections (1) and (2) of this section shall apply to a direction varying a previous direction under this section if and only if the varying direction extends the prices or charges to which this section applies or withdraws authority given under subsection (4)(*b*) of this section as respects the amount of any price or charge.

(8) If, by a sale of goods, or by the performance of services effected at a time when the direction under this section is in force, any person contravenes subsection (4) of this section he shall be liable—

(*a*)   on summary conviction to a fine not exceeding one hundred pounds, and

(*b*)   on conviction on indictment to a fine which, if the offender is not a body corporate, shall not exceed five hundred pounds.

BRINGING OF THIS PART INTO FORCE
> See s. 25, *ante.*

NOTICE
> The giving of notices is to be governed by regulations made under s. 21, *ante,* as applied by s. 25 (6), *ante.*

WRITING
> See the note " Written " to s. 7, *ante.*

20TH JULY 1966
> This was the date upon which the Prime Minister stated in the House of Commons that the Government were calling for a six-month standstill on wages, salaries and other types of income, followed by a further six months of severe restraint, and for a similar standstill on prices (see 732 H. of C. Official Report 636).

SELLING OF GOODS
> This Act applies to conditional sale agreements and hire-purchase agreements in accordance with s. 34 (3), *post*.

PERIOD . . . WITHIN WHICH, ETC.
> Cf. the note " Within three months " to s. 5, *ante*.

SHALL NOT EXCEED
> As to recovery of any excess over the lawful amount, see s. 33 (1), *post*.

IF . . . ANY PERSON CONTRAVENES, ETC.
> The general provisions as to offences contained in s. 22, *ante*, are applied by s. 25 (6), *ante*; note also the savings in s. 25 (4), (5), *ante*.

FINE
> See the note to s. 11, *ante*.

DEFINITIONS
> For " business ", " goods ", " Minister " and " price ", see s. 34 (1), *post*.

28. Restrictions on pay increases.—(1) The Secretary of State may by order apply this section to remuneration under contracts of employment for any kind of work to be performed wholly or substantially within the United Kingdom or on British ships or aircraft.

(2) An employer shall not pay remuneration to which this section applies at a rate which exceeds the rate of remuneration paid by him for the same kind of work before the date of the coming into force of the order applying this section to that description of remuneration by any amount unless the appropriate Minister has given his consent in writing to the increase of the remuneration by that amount, or by a greater amount.

(3) If an employer contravenes this section he shall be liable—

(*a*) on summary conviction to a fine not exceeding one hundred pounds, and

(*b*) on conviction on indictment to a fine which, if the offender is not a body corporate, shall not exceed five hundred pounds.

(4) Subsections (4), (5) and (6) of section 16 of this Act shall apply in relation to the payment of remuneration by an employer which would be in contravention of this or the next following section as they apply in relation to the implementation by an employer of an award or settlement which would be in contravention of the said section 16.

(5) Although this Part of this Act does not bind the Crown, an order may be made under this or the next following section, so as, without imposing any obligation on the Crown as an employer or otherwise, to apply (either expressly or impliedly) to persons employed by or under the Crown, and the said subsections (4), (5) and (6) of section 16 of this Act as extended by the last foregoing subsection, shall apply accordingly.

References in this subsection to employment by or under the Crown shall be construed in accordance with subsections (3) and (4) of section 18 of this Act.

(6) Section 17 of this Act shall apply as if references to Part II of this Act included references to this Part of this Act.

(7) An order under subsection (1) above may frame the descriptions of remuneration to which this section applies in any way, and in particular—

(*a*) may apply this section in relation to employees in specified kinds of work, or in specified localities, or working in specified undertakings or for specified employers,

(*b*) in applying it in relation to employees working in specified undertakings or for specified employers, may make distinctions as regards those undertakings and persons by reference to the regions or localities where the undertakers or employers carry on business, or the number of employees working in the undertakings or for the employers, or by reference to any other different circumstances, and may be made so as to apply to named undertakings or persons.

BRINGING OF THIS PART INTO FORCE
See s. 25, *ante.*

UNITED KINGDOM
See the note to s. 9, *ante.*

BRITISH SHIPS OR AIRCRAFT
For the ships which are deemed to be " British ships ", see the Merchant Shipping Act 1894 (23 Halsbury's Statutes (2nd Edn.) 411). As to " British aircraft ", see, *e.g.*, the definition in the Emergency Laws (Re-enactments and Repeals) Act 1964, s. 9 (2) (44 Halsbury's Statutes (2nd Edn.) 1343).

SHALL NOT PAY REMUNERATION . . . AT A RATE WHICH EXCEEDS, ETC.
The restriction imposed by sub-s. (2) must be read in the light of any provision made by virtue of s. 25 (7), (8), *ante.* Remuneration which has been unlawfully paid may not be recovered; see s. 33 (2), *post.*

WRITING
See the note " Written " to s. 7, *ante.*

IF AN EMPLOYER CONTRAVENES, ETC.
The general provisions as to offences contained in s. 22, *ante*, are applied by s. 25 (6), *ante*; note also the savings in s. 25 (4), (5), *ante.*
     As to offences, etc., see also s. 16 (4)–(6), *ante*, as applied by sub-s. (4) of this section.

FINE
See the note to s. 11, *ante.*

DOES NOT BIND THE CROWN
See the note to s. 18, *ante.*

DEFINITIONS
For " appropriate Minister " and " awards and settlements ", see s. 34 (1), *post* (and see also, as to " the appropriate Minister ", s. 25 (6), *ante*).

ORDERS UNDER THIS SECTION
No order had been made under sub-s. (1) up to 15th August 1966.
For general provisions as to orders made under this Part of the Act, see s. 25 (2), (5), *ante*.

29. Restrictions on pay by reference to levels at 20th July 1966.—
(1) The Secretary of State may give notice, published in the Gazette, that he is considering the making of an order under this section.

(2) A notice under subsection (1) above shall give particulars of the order proposed to be made, and shall specify a period, which shall be not less than fourteen days from the first publication of the notice, within which any employer, or any employers' organisation, trade union, trade union organisation or other person representing employers or employees may make representations in writing to the Secretary of State.

(3) The Secretary of State may, if he thinks fit, after the expiration of the period specified in the notice for the making of representations, and after considering any representations duly made, by order apply this section to remuneration under contracts of employment for any kind of work.

(4) An employer shall not pay remuneration to which this section applies for work for any period while the order is in force at a rate which exceeds the rate of remuneration paid by him for the same kind of work before 20th July 1966 by any amount unless—

(a) the appropriate Minister has given his consent in writing to an excess of that amount or of a greater amount, or

(b) the order authorises an excess of that amount, or of a greater amount.

(5) If an employer contravenes this section he shall be liable—

(a) on summary conviction to a fine not exceeding one hundred pounds, and

(b) on conviction on indictment to a fine which, if the offender is not a body corporate, shall not exceed five hundred pounds.

(6) An order under subsection (1) above may frame the descriptions of remuneration to which this section applies in any way and in particular may contain provisions corresponding to those authorised by paragraphs (a) and (b) of subsection (7) of the last foregoing section.

BRINGING OF THIS PART INTO FORCE
See s. 25, *ante*.

PERIOD . . . WITHIN WHICH, ETC.
Cf. the note " Within three months " to s. 5, *ante*.

FIRST PUBLICATION OF THE NOTICE
This is to be construed in accordance with s. 34 (4), *post.*

WRITING
See the note " Written " to s. 7, *ante.*

SHALL NOT PAY REMUNERATION . . .   AT A RATE WHICH EXCEEDS, ETC.
The restriction imposed by sub-s. (4) must be read in the light of any provision
made by virtue of s. 25 (7), (8), *ante.* Remuneration which has been unlawfully
paid may not be recovered; see s. 33 (2), *post.*

20TH JULY 1966
See the note to s. 27, *ante.*

IF AN EMPLOYER CONTRAVENES, ETC.
The general provisions as to offences contained in s. 22, *ante,* are applied by
s. 25 (6), *ante*; note also the savings in s. 25 (4), (5), *ante.*
    As to offences, etc., see also s. 16 (4)–(6), *ante,* as applied by s. 28 (4), *ante.*

FINE
See the note to s. 11, *ante.*

ORDER UNDER SUBSECTION (1)
It would appear that these words in sub-s. (6) should read " order under
subsection (3) ".

EMPLOYMENT UNDER THE CROWN
See s. 28 (5), *ante.*

DEFINITIONS
For " appropriate Minister ", see s. 34 (1), *post* (and see also s. 25 (6), *ante*);
for " trade union ", see (by virtue of s. 34 (1), *post*) the Trade Union Act 1913,
s. 2 (1) (25 Halsbury's Statutes (2nd Edn.) 1271); for " Gazette ", see s. 34 (4),
post.

ORDERS UNDER THIS SECTION
No order had been made under sub-s. (3) up to 15th August 1966.
    For general provisions as to orders made under this Part, see s. 25 (2),
(5), *ante.*

**30. Authority for employers to disregard pay increases in existing
contracts.**—(1) This section applies to any contract of employment
made before the date of the coming into force of this Part of this Act
under which any person who has worked for the employer since before
that date is to receive remuneration for the same kind of work for any
period after that date which is at a higher rate than that at which he was
being remunerated for work of that kind immediately before that date.

(2) If after having given not less than one week's notice in writing,
the employer pays or tenders to the employee remuneration for work
for any period after the said date and while this Part of this Act is in
force at a rate which is not less than that at which he was paid for the
same kind of work immediately before that date, the employer shall not
be liable in respect of a breach of a contract to which this section applies
for failure to pay remuneration at the rate provided by the contract.

(3) Subsection (2) above shall not take away the employee's right
to rescind the contract.

(4) The Secretary of State may by regulations in a statutory instrument make provision for the purposes of this section, as it applies to any work specified in the regulations, corresponding to the provision which may be made by an order under this Part of this Act in pursuance of section 25(8) of this Act.

(5) This section shall not apply to a contract for work to be performed wholly or mainly outside the United Kingdom.

BRINGING OF THIS PART INTO FORCE
See s. 25, *ante*.

NOT LESS THAN ONE WEEK'S NOTICE
I.e., at least seven days must elapse between the day on which the notice is given and that on which the remuneration in question is paid or tendered; see, in particular, *R.* v. *Turner*, [1910] 1 K.B. 346; *Re Hector Whaling, Ltd.*, [1936] Ch. 208; [1935] All E.R. Rep. 302; and *Thompson* v. *Stimpson*, [1960] 3 All E.R. 500; [1961] 1 Q.B. 195.

WRITING
See the note " Written " to s. 7, *ante*.

EMPLOYEE
For meaning, see s. 34 (1), *post*.

STATUTORY INSTRUMENT
For provisions as to statutory instruments generally, see the Statutory Instruments Act 1946 (24 Halsbury's Statutes (2nd Edn.) 440).

WHOLLY OR MAINLY
As to the meaning of the expression (or of the expression " exclusively or mainly "), see *Re Hatschak's Patents, Ex parte Zerenner*, [1909] 2 Ch. 68; *Miller* v. *Ottilie (Owners)*, [1944] 1 All E.R. 277; [1944] K.B. 188; and *Berthelemy* v. *Neale*, [1952] 1 All E.R. 437, C.A. See also *Franklin* v. *Gramophone Co., Ltd.*, [1948] 1 All E.R. 353; [1948] 1 K.B. 542, C.A., at p. 358 and p. 555, respectively, per Somervell, L.J.

UNITED KINGDOM
See the note to s. 9, *ante*.

REGULATIONS UNDER THIS SECTION
No regulations had been made under sub-s. (4) up to 15th August 1966.
As to the making of regulations before this Part of the Act is brought into force, see s. 25 (2), *ante*.

31. Wages regulation orders under Wages Councils Act 1959.—
(1) So long as this Part of this Act is in force, section 11(4) of the Wages Councils Act 1959 shall not impose a duty on the Minister of Labour (in this section called " the Minister ") to make an order giving effect to any wages regulation proposals, and the making of such an order, and the date to be specified in such an order for the coming into operation of the proposals, shall be at the Minister's discretion.

(2) The Minister may, by an order which is made under the said section 11(4) at a time when this Part of this Act is in force, and which

gives effect to wages regulation proposals which include provisions for fixing remuneration, being provisions expressed to take effect on a date specified in those proposals, direct that those provisions shall take effect at such later date as is specified in the order.

(3) The Minister may by an order which is made at a time when this Part of this Act is in force direct—

(a) that any wages regulation proposals to which effect is given by an order under the said section 11(4) shall take effect on such date as is specified in the order under this section, being a date other than the date specified in the order under the said section 11(4), or

(b) in the case of an order under the said section 11(4) which gives effect to proposals including such provisions as are described in subsection (2) above, that those provisions shall take effect at such date as is specified in the order, being a date other than the date specified in those provisions,

but so that an order under paragraph (a) or (b) above shall not affect provisions which have taken effect before the making of the order.

(4) The Minister shall not exercise his discretion under subsection (1) above so as to postpone the coming into operation of any wages regulation proposals to a date after the end of the twelve month period mentioned in subsection (1) of section 25 of this Act, or under subsection (2) or subsection (3) above specify a date after the end of that period, and if under the said section 25 this Part of this Act ceases to have effect at a date before the end of that twelve month period, the Minister shall by order under this section make such provision as appears to him expedient for producing the result which would have been secured by the foregoing provisions of this subsection if that date had been the end of the said twelve month period.

(5) An order made under this section—

(a) shall be contained in a statutory instrument, and

(b) may be varied or revoked by a subsequent order so made,

and any provisions included in an order under section 11(4) of the Wages Councils Act 1959 by virtue of subsection (2) of this section may be varied by an order made by the Minister under this section.

(6) This section shall have effect as respects Northern Ireland—

(a) with the substitution for references to the Minister of Labour, the Wages Councils Act 1959 and section 11 (4) of that Act, of references to the Ministry of Health and Social Services for Northern Ireland, the Wages Councils Act (Northern Ireland) 1945 and section 10 (4) of that Act, respectively; and

(b) with the omission of subsection (4) (a).

BRINGING OF THIS PART INTO FORCE
See s. 25, *ante*.

WAGES REGULATION PROPOSALS
This expression is defined by the Wages Councils Act 1959, s. 11 (1) (39 Halsbury's Statutes (2nd Edn.) 315).

STATUTORY INSTRUMENTS
See the note to s. 30, *ante*.

WAGES COUNCILS ACT 1959, s. 11 (4)
See 39 Halsbury's Statutes (2nd Edn.) 316.

WAGES COUNCILS ACT (NORTHERN IRELAND) 1945
1945 c. 21 (N.I.).

ORDERS UNDER THIS SECTION
No order had been made under sub-s. (3) or (4), or by virtue of sub-s. (2), of this section up to 15th August 1966.

32. Orders under Agricultural Wages Act 1948.—(1) The Minister of Agriculture, Fisheries and Food may, by an order made at a time when this Part of this Act is in force, direct that any order made by the Agricultural Wages Board under section 3, section 6 or section 7 of the Agricultural Wages Act 1948 (orders fixing rates of wages and holidays and dealing with related matters) shall not have effect until such date as is specified in the order under this section but so that an order under this subsection shall not affect provisions which have taken effect before the making of the order.

(2) The Minister shall not under subsection (1) above specify a date after the end of the twelve month period mentioned in subsection (1) of section 25 of this Act, and if under the said section 25 this Part of this Act ceases to have effect at a date before the end of that twelve month period, the Minister shall revoke any order under this section which is then in force.

(3) An order made under this section—

(*a*) shall be contained in a statutory instrument, and

(*b*) may be varied or revoked by a subsequent order so made.

(4) This section shall have effect as respects Scotland with the substitution—

(*a*) for references to the Minister of Agriculture, Fisheries and Food, of references to the Secretary of State;

(*b*) for references to the Agricultural Wages Board, of references to the Scottish Agricultural Wages Board; and

(*c*) for references to the Agricultural Wages Act 1948 and to sections 3, 6 or 7 of that Act, of references respectively to

[*46*]

the Agricultural Wages (Scotland) Act 1949 and to sections 3, 6 and 7 of that Act.

(5) This section shall have effect as respect Northern Ireland—

(*a*) with the substitution for references to the Minister of Agriculture, Fisheries and Food, the Agricultural Wages Board, the Agricultural Wages Act 1948 and section 3 of that Act, of references to the Ministry of Agriculture for Northern Ireland, the Agricultural Wages Board for Northern Ireland, the Agricultural Wages (Regulation) Act (Northern Ireland) 1939 and section 2 of that Act respectively; and

(*b*) with the omission of references to sections 6 and 7 of the said Act of 1948 and of subsection (4) (*a*).

BRINGING OF THIS PART INTO FORCE
See s. 25, *ante.*

AGRICULTURAL WAGES BOARD
This board is established by the Agricultural Wages Act 1948, s. 1, Sch. 1 (28 Halsbury's Statutes (2nd Edn.) 3, 19).

STATUTORY INSTRUMENT
See the note to s. 30, *ante.*

AGRICULTURAL WAGES ACT 1948, SS. 3, 6, 7
See 28 Halsbury's Statutes (2nd Edn.) 5, 9, 11.

AGRICULTURAL WAGES (SCOTLAND) ACT 1949
12, 13 & 14 Geo. 6 c. 30.

AGRICULTURAL WAGES (REGULATION) ACT (NORTHERN IRELAND) 1939
2 & 3 Geo. 6 c. 25 (N.I.).

ORDERS UNDER THIS SECTION
No order had been made under sub-s. (1) up to 15th August 1966.

33. Illegal transactions.—(1) A transaction shall not be invalid in consequence of the provisions of section 26 or 27 of this Act, but the person paying any price or charge which is unlawful under the provisions of either of those sections may recover the part of it in excess of the lawful amount unless he is a person who is himself liable to punishment by reason of his having aided, abetted, or counselled or procured the offence committed under those provisions by the other party to the transaction.

(2) An employer shall not under any circumstances be entitled, in consequence of the provisions of this Part of this Act relating to contracts of employment, to recover any remuneration which he has paid.

BRINGING OF THIS PART INTO FORCE
See s. 25, *ante.*

AIDED, ABETTED, OR COUNSELLED OR PROCURED THE OFFENCE
A person who aids, abets, counsels or procures the commission of such an offence may be proceeded against as if he were a principal offender under the Accessories and Abettors Act 1861, s. 8 (5 Halsbury's Statutes (2nd Edn.) 726), or the Magistrates' Courts Act 1952, s. 35 (32 Halsbury's Statutes (2nd Edn.) 451).

PROVISIONS OF THIS PART . . . RELATING TO CONTRACTS OF EMPLOYMENT
See, in particular, ss. 28 and 29, *ante.*

PART V

GENERAL

34. Interpretation.—(1) In this Act, unless the context otherwise requires:—

" appropriate Minister " shall be construed in accordance with regulations made under section 21 of this Act;

" awards and settlements ", in relation to terms or conditions of employment, includes any agreement, whether or not enforceable in law and whether or not concluded under recognised arrangements for the settlement by negotiations of terms and conditions of employment, to which any employer or any organisation representing employers is a party;

" business " in the expression " in the course of business " includes any trade, profession or vocation;

" employee " means an individual who has entered into or works under a contract with an employer, whether the contract be for manual labour, clerical work or otherwise, be expressed or implied, oral or in writing, and whether it be a contract of service or of apprenticeship; and cognate expressions shall be construed accordingly;

" goods " includes ships and aircraft, minerals, substances and animals (including fish);

" Minister " has the same meaning as " Minister of the Crown " in the Ministers of the Crown (Transfer of Functions) Act 1946;

" price " includes a charge of any description;

" public notice " includes any notice given by any member of a trade association to other members of that trade association;

" trade association " means any body of persons (whether incorporated or not) which is formed for the purpose of furthering the trade interests of its members or of the persons represented by its members;

" trade union " has the meaning given by the Trade Union Act 1913.

(2) Any reference in this Act to any other enactment shall, except

so far as the context otherwise requires, be construed as a reference to that enactment as amended or applied by or under any other enactment, including this Act.

(3) This Act shall apply in relation to—

(a) a conditional sale agreement, and

(b) a hire-purchase agreement,

as if the agreement were a sale of the goods to which the agreement relates for an amount equal to the total purchase price or hire-purchase price with a fair reduction where the consideration for receipt of that price includes the installation, maintenance or repair of the goods or the performance of other services apart from the giving of credit.

This subsection shall be construed, except as it applies in Scotland, in accordance with the Hire-Purchase Act 1965 and, as it applies in Scotland, in accordance with the Hire-Purchase (Scotland) Act 1965.

(4) In this Act " Gazette " means, in relation to a matter relating exclusively to England and Wales, or exclusively to Scotland, or exclusively to Northern Ireland, the London Gazette, the Edinburgh Gazette and the Belfast Gazette respectively, similarly for matters to be published or notified in any two of those Gazettes, and, subject to that, all three of those Gazettes; and, where anything is under this Act to be published or notified in more than one of those Gazettes, and is so published or notified on different dates, references in this Act to the date on which it is published or notified in the Gazette are references to the earlier or earliest of those dates.

EMPLOYEE
   This definition is identical with the definition of " employee " in the Contracts of Employment Act 1963, s. 8 (1) (43 Halsbury's Statutes (2nd Edn.) 283).

WRITING
   See the note " Written " to s. 7, *ante*.

TRADE ASSOCIATION
   This definition is virtually identical with the definition of " trade association " in the Restrictive Trade Practices Act 1956, s. 6 (8) (36 Halsbury's Statutes (2nd Edn.) 938).

DEFINITIONS
   By virtue of the second paragraph of sub-s. (3), for " conditional sale agreement " and " hire-purchase agreement ", see the Hire-Purchase Act 1965, s. 1 (1) (45 Halsbury's Statutes (2nd Edn.) 1416), and for " hire-purchase price " and " total purchase price ", see s. 58 (1), (2) of that Act (45 Halsbury's Statutes (2nd Edn.) 1460, 1461); by virtue of the said paragraph and s. 58 (1) of the Act of 1965 (45 Halsbury's Statutes (2nd Edn.) 1460), for " goods " and " sale ", see the Sale of Goods Act 1893, s. 62 (1) (22 Halsbury's Statutes (2nd Edn.) 1018).

MINISTERS OF THE CROWN (TRANSFER OF FUNCTIONS) ACT 1946
   By s. 8 (2) of that Act (4 Halsbury's Statutes (2nd Edn.) 563), as amended by the Defence (Transfer of Functions) (No. 1) Order 1964, S.I. 1964 No. 488, art. 2, Sch. 1, Part I, the expression " Minister of the Crown " means the

holder of an office in Her Majesty's Government in the United Kingdom, and includes the Treasury, the Board of Trade and the Defence Council.

TRADE UNION ACT 1913
By s. 2 (1) of that Act (25 Halsbury's Statutes (2nd Edn.) 1271), the expression " trade union " means any combination, whether temporary or permanent, the principal objects of which are under its constitution statutory objects, but any combination which is registered as a trade union is to be deemed to be a trade union as defined by the Act of 1913 so long as it continues to be so registered; and by s. 1 (2) of that Act (25 Halsbury's Statutes (2nd Edn.) 1270), the expression " statutory objects " means the objects mentioned in the Trade Union Act Amendment Act 1876, s. 16 (25 Halsbury's Statutes (2nd Edn.) 1263), namely, the regulation of the relations between workmen and masters, or between workmen and workmen, or between masters and masters, or the imposing of restrictive conditions on the conduct of any trade or business, and also the provision of benefits to members.

HIRE-PURCHASE ACT 1965
See 45 Halsbury's Statutes (2nd Edn.) 1414.

HIRE-PURCHASE (SCOTLAND) ACT 1965
1965 c. 67.

35. Administrative expenses.—Any administrative expenses incurred by a government department in consequence of the provisions of this Act may be paid out of money provided by Parliament.

36. Application to Northern Ireland.—It is hereby declared that this Act extends to Northern Ireland, but the Parliament of Northern Ireland shall have the same power to pass Acts with respect to any matter as they would have had if this Act had not passed and, in the event of any inconsistency between any Act of the Parliament of Northern Ireland duly passed after the passing of this Act and any provision of this Act, the Act of the Parliament of Northern Ireland shall, in Northern Ireland, prevail.

PASSING OF THIS ACT
This Act was passed (*i.e.*, received the Royal Assent) on 12th August 1966.

37. Short title.—This Act may be cited as the Prices and Incomes Act 1966.

SCHEDULES

SCHEDULE 1   Section 1

INCIDENTAL PROVISIONS WITH RESPECT TO THE BOARD

1. The Board shall be a body corporate with perpetual succession and a common seal.

THE BOARD
    I.e., the National Board for Prices and Incomes; see s. 1 (1), *ante.*

BODY CORPORATE
    For the general law relating to corporations, see 9 Halsbury's Laws (3rd Edn.) 3 *et seq.*

Tenure of office, etc., of members

2.—(1) Subject to the following provisions of this paragraph, a member of the Board shall hold and vacate office as such in accordance with the terms of his appointment.

(2) A person shall not be appointed to the Board for a term exceeding five years, but previous membership thereof shall not affect eligibility for re-appointment.

(3) The Secretary of State may, with the consent of the member concerned, vary the terms of appointment of any member of the Board so as to provide for him to serve as a full-time member instead of as a part-time member or, as the case may be, as a part-time member instead of as a full-time member.

(4) A member of the Board may at any time resign his membership by notice in writing addressed to the Secretary of State.

(5) The Secretary of State may, by notice in writing addressed to the member in question, terminate the appointment of any member of the Board who is, in his opinion, unfit to continue in office or incapable of performing his duties as a member.

THE BOARD
    I.e., the National Board for Prices and Incomes; see s. 1 (1), *ante.*

WRITING
    See the note " Written " to s. 7, *ante.*

Tenure of office of chairman and deputies

3.—(1) Subject to the following provisions of this paragraph, the chairman and any deputy chairman of the Board shall hold and vacate office as such in accordance with the terms of his appointment.

(2) The chairman or a deputy chairman of the Board may at any time resign his office as such by notice in writing addressed to the Secretary of State.

(3) If the chairman or a deputy chairman of the Board ceases to be a member, or a full-time member, of the Board, he shall also cease to be chairman or, as the case may be, a deputy chairman.

THE BOARD
I.e., the National Board for Prices and Incomes; see s. 1 (1), *ante*.

WRITING
See the note " Written " to s. 7, *ante*.

Application of House of Commons Disqualification Act

4. In Part II of Schedule 1 to the House of Commons Disqualification Act 1957 (bodies of which all members are disqualified under that Act), there shall (at the appropriate place in alphabetical order) be inserted the following entry:—
" The National Board for Prices and Incomes ";
and the like amendment shall be made in the Part substituted for the said Part II by Schedule 3 to that Act in its application to the Senate and House of Commons of Northern Ireland.

HOUSE OF COMMONS DISQUALIFICATION ACT 1957, SCH. 1, PART II, SCH. 3
See 37 Halsbury's Statutes (2nd Edn.) 854, 863.

Officers and servants

5. The Board shall have a secretary, to be appointed by them after consultation with the Secretary of State, and may, after consultation with the Secretary of State and with the consent of the Treasury, appoint such other officers and servants as they think fit.

6. The Board shall pay to their officers and servants such remuneration, and such travelling and other allowances, as the Secretary of State may with the approval of the Treasury determine.

THE BOARD
I.e., the National Board for Prices and Incomes; see s. 1 (1), *ante*.

CONSULTATION
See the note " Consult " to s. 4, *ante*.

General provisions with respect to the Board's proceedings

7. The validity of any proceedings of the Board shall not be affected by any vacancy among the members of the Board, or by any defect in the appointment of any such member.

8. Subject to paragraph 15 below, the Board may determine their own procedure, including the quorum necessary for their meetings.

THE BOARD
I.e., the National Board for Prices and Incomes; see s. 1 (1), *ante*.

QUORUM
" The word ' quorum ' in its ordinary signification, has reference to the existence of a complete body of persons, of whom a certain specified number are competent to transact the business of the whole. But a quorum of a board of directors does not constitute the board, though, in the absence of other existing directors, it may legally transact such business as the whole board is competent to transact "; see *Faure Electric Accumulator Co., Ltd.* v. *Phillipart* (1888), 58 L.T. 525, at p. 527, *per* Hawkins, J.

Exercise of chairman's functions during absence, incapacity etc.

9.—(1) At any time when the chairman of the Board is absent or otherwise incapable of acting, or there is a vacancy in the office of chairman—

(a) such one of the Board's deputy chairmen as the Secretary of State may direct or, in default of any such direction, such one of them as they may agree, or

(b) if there is then only one deputy chairman of the Board, the deputy chairman,

may exercise any of the functions of chairman of the Board.

(2) At any time when every person who is chairman or deputy chairman of the Board is absent or otherwise incapable of acting, or there is no such person, such member of the Board as the Secretary of State may direct or, in default of any such direction, such member of the Board as the Board may agree may exercise any of the functions of chairman of the Board.

THE BOARD
   I.e., the National Board for Prices and Incomes; see s. 1 (1), *ante*.

Remission of questions for preliminary examination by groups of members and persons specially appointed

10.—(1) A question referred to the Board under section 2 of this Act, or any matter to be considered by the Board in pursuance of an instruction or requirement under section 3 of this Act, shall, if the chairman so directs, be examined, before consideration by the Board, by a group of persons consisting of—

(a) not less than three members of the Board nominated by him, and

(b) such other persons, if any, as he may think fit to nominate for the purpose, being persons drawn in equal numbers from the panels maintained by the Secretary of State pursuant to paragraph 11 below;

and in any such case, the Board, in formulating any report, shall take into consideration, but shall not be bound to accept, any findings or recommendations of the group.

(2) Where such a direction is given as respects a matter to be examined in pursuance of an instruction or requirement under section 3 of this Act, and any member of the Board is, by the terms of his appointment, appointed to deal specially with matters which include the subject matter of the instruction, he shall be one of the said group of persons.

11.—(1) For the purposes of paragraph 10 above, the Secretary of State shall draw up, and from time to time revise, two panels, one of persons appearing to him to have special knowledge or experience of matters concerning employers, and the other of persons appearing to him to have special knowledge or experience of matters concerning employees.

(2) In the exercise of his functions under the foregoing subparagraph, the Secretary of State shall consult with such organisations as he may consider appropriate, being organisations which appear to him to be representative of employers or, as the case may be, employees.

(3) The Board may if they think fit pay to persons whose names are included in either of the said panels such travelling and other allowances as the Secretary of State may with the approval of the Treasury determine.

12.—(1) The chairman of the Board shall nominate as chairman of any group constituted for the purposes of paragraph 10 above one of the members of the group who are also members of the Board.

(2) Where during the proceedings of any such group any member thereof ceases to be a member of the Board, or the name of any such member is removed from either of the said panels, he shall cease to be a member of the group, and the chairman of the Board shall appoint in his place another member of the Board or, as the case may be, another person drawn from the panel in question.

(3) Where during the proceedings of any such group the chairman of the Board is satisfied that any member of the group will be unable for a substantial period to perform his duties as such, he may if he thinks fit appoint in the place of that member another member of the Board or, as the case may be, another person drawn from the panel from which that member was drawn.

(4) Subject to paragraph 15 below, and to any specific or general directions which may from time to time be given by the Board, any such group may determine their own procedure, including the quorum necessary for their meetings.

CONSULT
See the note to s. 4, *ante.*

QUORUM
See the note to paras. 7 and 8 of this Schedule, *ante.*

DEFINITIONS
For " the Board ", see s. 1 (1), *ante*; for " employee ", see s. 34 (1), *ante.*

Inquiries

13.—(1) The Board, and any group constituted under paragraph 10 above, may hold such inquiries as they consider necessary or desirable for the discharge of their functions under this Act; and the chairman of the Board or, as the case may be, group, or other member of the Board presiding in his stead, may at any such inquiry direct that any person appearing as a witness be examined on oath, and administer an oath accordingly, or, instead of so directing, require the person examined to make and subscribe a declaration of the truth of the matter respecting which he is examined.

(2) If any person who is to give evidence at any such inquiry so requests at the hearing, or by a notice in writing served on the Board's secretary before the date of the hearing, the public shall be excluded from the hearing while that person gives his evidence.

14.—(1) For the purposes of any inquiry under this Act, the chairman of the Board or, as the case may be, group, or any other member of the Board authorised by the chairman of the Board (whether generally or in connection with the particular inquiry) to exercise the powers conferred by this sub-paragraph, may by summons—

(*a*) require any person to attend, at such time and place as is specified in the summons, to give evidence on, or to produce all documents in his possession or control which relate to, any matter so specified, being a matter in question at the inquiry, or

(*b*) require any person carrying on any trade or business, or any trade union or trade association or officer of a trade union or trade association, to furnish to the Board or group such estimates, returns or other information as may be specified or described in the summons, and specify the time, the manner and the form in which any such estimates, returns or information are to be furnished.

(2) No person shall be compelled for the purposes of any such inquiry to give any evidence or produce any document which he could not be compelled to give or produce in proceedings before the High Court or, in complying with any requirement for the furnishing of information, to give any information which he could not be compelled to give in evidence in such proceedings.

(3) No person shall be required, in obedience to a summons under this paragraph to go more than ten miles from his place of residence unless the necessary expenses of his attendance are paid or tendered to him.

(4) A person who—

(*a*) refuses or wilfully neglects to attend in obedience to a summons issued under this paragraph, or to give evidence as required by such a summons, or

(*b*) wilfully alters, suppresses, conceals, destroys or refuses to produce any book or other document which he has been required to produce by such a summons, or

(*c*) refuses or wilfully neglects to furnish any estimate, return or other information required of him by such a summons or, in furnishing any such estimate, return or other information, makes any statement which he knows to be false in a material particular, or recklessly makes any statement which is false in a material particular,

shall be liable on summary conviction to a fine not exceeding fifty pounds.

(5) Proceedings for an offence under the last foregoing sub-paragraph may (without prejudice to any jurisdiction exercisable apart from this sub-paragraph) be taken against a body corporate at any place at which the body has a place of business, against a trade union or trade association at the place at which it has its head office, and against any other person at any place at which he is for the time being; and subsections (2), (3) and (5) of section 22 of this Act shall apply in relation to such an offence as they apply in relation to an offence under Part II of this Act, but as if, in those subsections any reference to a trade union included a reference to any trade association which is not a corporation.

(6) In the application of this paragraph to Scotland, for any reference to a summons there shall be substituted a reference to a notice in writing, and for the reference to the High Court there shall be substituted a reference to the Court of Session; and in the application of this paragraph to Northern

Ireland, for the reference to the High Court there shall be substituted a reference to the High Court in Northern Ireland.

OATH

This includes, in the case of persons allowed by law to affirm or declare instead of swearing, affirmation and declaration; see the Interpretation Act 1889, s. 3 (24 Halsbury's Statutes (2nd Edn.) 207) (note also the provision concerning declarations made by the above para. 13 (1)).

WRITING

See the note " Written " to s. 7, *ante*.

TEN MILES

Quaere whether, by virtue of the Interpretation Act 1889, s. 34 (24 Halsbury's Statutes (2nd Edn.) 226), this is to be measured in a straight line on a horizontal plane.

WILFULLY

This expression, in the words of Lord Russell of Killowen, C.J., in *R.* v. *Senior*, [1899] 1 Q.B. 283, at pp. 290, 291, "means that the act is done deliberately and intentionally, not by accident or inadvertence, but so that the mind of the person who does the act goes with it "; see also, in particular, *R.* v. *Walker*, [1934], 24 Cr. App. Rep. 117; *Eaton* v. *Cobb*, [1950] 1 All E.R. 1016; and *Arrowsmith* v. *Jenkins*, [1963] 2 All E.R. 210; [1963] 2 Q.B. 561.

KNOWS

There is authority for saying that, where a person deliberately refrains from making inquiries the results of which he might not care to have, this constitutes in law actual knowledge of the facts in question; see *Knox* v. *Boyd*, 1941 S.C. (J.) 82, at p. 86, and *Taylor's Central Garages (Exeter), Ltd.* v. *Roper* (1951), J.P. 445, at pp. 449, 450, *per* Devlin, J.; and see also, in particular, *Mallon* v. *Allon*, [1963] 3 All E.R. 843; [1964] 1 Q.B. 385, at p. 847 and p. 394, respectively. However, mere neglect to ascertain what would have been found out by making reasonable enquiries is not tantamount to knowledge; see *Taylor's Central Garages (Exeter), Ltd.* v. *Roper, ubi supra, per* Devlin, J.; and cf. *London Computator, Ltd.* v. *Seymour*, [1944] 2 All E.R. 11; but see also *Mallon* v. *Allon, ubi supra.*

FALSE

A statement may be false on account of what it omits even though it is literally true; see *R.* v. *Kylsant (Lord)*, [1932] 1 K.B. 442; [1931] All E.R. Rep. 179; and *R.* v. *Bishirgian*, [1936] 1 All E.R. 586; and cf. *Curtis* v. *Chemical Cleaning and Dyeing Co., Ltd.*, [1951] 1 All E.R. 631; [1951] 1 K.B. 805, C.A., at p. 634 and pp. 808, 809 respectively, *per* Denning, L.J. Whether or not any advantage accrues from the false statement is immaterial; see *Jones* v. *Meatyard*, [1939] 1 All E.R. 140 and *Stevens & Steeds, Ltd. and Evans* v. *King*, [1943] 1 All E.R. 314.

MATERIAL PARTICULAR

A particular may be material on the mere ground that it renders more credible something else; see *R.* v. *Tyson* (1867), L.R. 1 C.C.R. 107.

RECKLESSLY

On the meaning of this expression, see, in particular, *Derry* v. *Peek* (1889), 14 App. Cas. 337; [1886-90] All E.R. Rep. 1; *Williams Brothers Direct Supply Stores, Ltd.* v. *Cloote* (1944), 60 T.L.R. 270; *R.* v. *Bates*, [1952] 2 All E.R. 842; on appeal *sub nom. R.* v. *Russell*, [1953] 1 W.L.R. 77; 97 Sol. Jo. 12; *R.* v. *Mackinnon*, [1958] 3 All E.R. 657; [1959] 1 Q.B. 150; and *R.* v. *Grunwald*, [1960] 3 All E.R. 380; [1963] 1 Q.B. 935.

DEFINITIONS
> For " the Board ", see s. 1 (1), *ante*; for " trade association ", see s. 34 (1), *ante*; for " trade union ", see (by virtue of s. 34 (1), *ante*) the Trade Union Act 1913, s. 2 (1) (25 Halsbury's Statutes (2nd Edn.) 1271).

Power of Secretary of State to give procedural directions

15. In determining any matter of procedure (including the quorum necessary for their meetings), the Board and any group constituted under paragraph 10 above shall act in accordance with any general directions which may from time to time be given with respect thereto by the Secretary of State.

QUORUM
> See the note to paras. 7 and 8 of this Schedule, *ante*.

THE BOARD
> *I.e.*, the National Board for Prices and Incomes; see s. 1 (1), *ante*.

Disclosure of information

16.—(1) Subject to the following sub-paragraph, no information given or supplied by any person in connection with the examination of any question under this Act shall be disclosed except—

(a) with that person's consent, or

(b) to members of the Board and, so far as they are not members of the Board, of any group by whom the question is examined pursuant to paragraph 10 above, or

(c) to the Board's officers and servants, or

(d) to the Secretary of State, the President of the Board of Trade or any other Minister, or an officer or servant appointed by, or person exercising functions on behalf of, the Secretary of State, the President of the Board of Trade or any other Minister, or

(e) with a view to the institution of, or otherwise for the purposes of, any criminal proceedings pursuant to or arising out of this Act.

(2) The foregoing sub-paragraph does not apply to information given or supplied in any proceedings to which the public are admitted, or contained in any report of the Board as laid before Parliament, or published, pursuant to section 5(1) of this Act.

(3) Any person who discloses any information in contravention of sub-paragraph (1) above shall be liable on summary conviction to a fine not exceeding one hundred pounds or to imprisonment for a term not exceeding three months or both, or on conviction on indictment to a fine or to imprisonment for a term not exceeding two years or both.

(4) In paragraph (d) of that sub-paragraph " Minister " includes any Minister of the Government of Northern Ireland.

THREE MONTHS
> As the maximum term of imprisonment on summary conviction does not exceed three months, trial by jury may not be claimed under the Magistrates' Courts Act 1952, s. 25 (32 Halsbury's Statutes (2nd Edn.) 443).

FINE

There is no limit to the amount of the fine which may be imposed on indictment; but see 25 Edw. 1 (Magna Carta) (1297), c. 14 (4 Halsbury's Statutes (2nd Edn.) 24), and the Bill of Rights (1688) (Sess. 2 c. 2), s. 1 (4 Halsbury's Statutes (2nd Edn.) 152).

DEFINITIONS

For " the Board " see s. 1 (1), *ante*; for " Minister ", see s. 34 (1), *ante* (and note sub-para. (4) of this paragraph).

Expenses of the Board

17. The expenses incurred by the Board under paragraph 6, 11(3) or 14(3) above and, to such amount as the Secretary of State may with the approval of the Treasury determine, any other expenses of the Board shall be paid out of money provided by Parliament.

THE BOARD

I.e., the National Board for Prices and Incomes; see s. 1 (1), *ante*.

Section 4 SCHEDULE 2

PRICES AND INCOMES STANDSTILL

This Schedule incorporates into the Act the provisions of the White Paper of July 1966, " Prices and Incomes Standstill " (Cmnd. 3073). It is substituted by the Prices and Incomes (General Considerations) Order, 1966, made by the Secretary of State on 12th August, 1966 (S.I. 1966 No. 1021) by virtue of the powers given to him by s. 4 (2) of the Act. (The Schedule as originally enacted reproduced Part I of the White Paper of April 1965, " Prices and Incomes Policy (Cmnd. 2639), which may now be regarded as obsolete.) It sets out the considerations to which the National Board of Prices and Incomes is to have regard in examining questions referred to them under s. 2, *ante*, and in complying with any instruction or requirement under s. 3, *ante* (s. 4 (1), *ante*), and to which various persons and bodies are to have regard in exercising their functions under any enactment in connection with the regulation of prices or charges of any of the descriptions specified in Sch. 3, para. 2, *post* (s. 23 (1), *ante*). These considerations may be further added to or modified by order made under s. 4 (2), *ante*.

I. INTRODUCTION

In a statement in the House of Commons on 20th July 1966, the Prime Minister drew attention to the fact that money incomes have been increasing at a rate far faster than could be justified by increasing production, and called for a standstill on prices and incomes. Details of the way in which it is proposed that the standstill should be applied are set out in the paragraphs below.

2. The country needs a breathing space of twelve months in which productivity can catch up with the excessive increases in incomes which have been taking place. The broad intention is to secure in the first six months (which can be regarded, for convenience, as the period to the end of December 1966) a standstill in which increases in prices or in incomes will so far as possible be avoided altogether. The first half of 1967 will be regarded as a

period of severe restraint in which some increases may be justified where there are particularly compelling reasons for them, but exceptional restraint will be needed by all who are concerned with determining prices and incomes.

II. PRICES

3. The introduction of a general standstill on prices and charges until the end of 1966, to be followed by a six-month period of severe restraint, is intended to apply to prices of all goods and services, whether provided by private or public enterprise. All enterprises will be expected to make every effort to absorb increases in costs, whatever the circumstances in which these arise.

4. This standstill period will apply except to the limited extent that increases in prices or charges may be necessary because of marked increases which cannot be absorbed, in costs of imported materials, or which arise from changes in supply for seasonal or other reasons, or which are due to action by the Government such as increased taxation.

5. In some instances an enterprise may feel compelled to propose an increase in price where it finds it impracticable to absorb increased costs over which it cannot exercise full control (e.g. manufacturers whose products include a high proportion of bought-in components). Any such cases will be subject to the most rigorous scrutiny in the light of national economic needs, including the requirements of export trade.

6. The criteria for price increases appropriate throughout the whole period are thus much more stringent than those set out in the White Paper on Prices and Incomes Policy (Cmnd. 2639, Part I, paragraph 9). The criteria for price reductions set out in that White Paper (ibid. paragraph 10) will still apply.

Type of Price Covered

7. Although the paragraphs above relate primarily to manufacturers' prices for the home market, wholesalers and retailers have a duty no less to do everything possible, e.g. by not increasing cash margins, to avoid any increases in prices.

"Early Warning" arrangements for the Periods of Standstill and Severe Restraint

8. The "early warning" arrangements at present in force* are to continue. But the Government consider it essential that they should be extended to cover a wider field of items, and they will be consulting the Confederation of British Industry and other interested organisations about this.

9. In the meantime, however, the standstill applies equally to goods and services within and outside the present "early warning" system. Any manufacturing enterprise, other than those to which the exceptions in paragraph 10 below apply, which considers that it is justified in proposing a price

---

* White Paper on Prices and Incomes Policy: An "Early Warning" System (Cmnd. 2808).

increase on the grounds set out in paragraphs 4 and 5 above should notify the appropriate Government Department. It will be expected to make no increase in price without receiving written confirmation from the Government that no further standstill on the increase is required.

10. Prior notification is not required—

(*a*) in respect of increases in prices of the food items listed in Part B of the Appendix to Cmnd. 2808, which will continue to be kept under constant watch by the Ministry of Agriculture, Fisheries and Food in accordance with the terms of paragraph 5 of Cmnd. 2808;

(*b*) from enterprises which are not included in the "early warning" arrangements and which employ fewer than 100 workers.

Rents

11. The level of rents charged by landlords for virtually the whole of the private housing sector is already determined within the statutory framework of the Rent Acts, but the Government will keep under the closest scrutiny the movement of rents of private housing.

12. Local authority rents are already on a non-profit making and sub-sidised basis. If increased costs are not met from rents they must be recouped from rates, which are also a charge on tenants, local authority tenants paying the two—rent and rates—in a single payment. In the period of the prices standstill until the end of 1966 the Government expect local authorities to take such practical steps as are possible to prevent or postpone rent increases, including those already announced. Where, in consultation with the Minister of Housing and Local Government or the Secretary of State for Scotland, increases are deemed to be unavoidable, the Government hope that local authorities will make provision for the protection of tenants of limited means through rent rebate schemes. Similar considerations apply to rents of houses provided by other public authorities, e.g. New Towns.

Rents of Business Premises and of Land

13. In calling for a standstill on the prices of goods and services, the Government recognise that increases in the rents of business premises and of land have an effect on prices of goods and services. The principles of the standstill are expected to apply to all such rents no less than to the prices of goods and services, and landlords should take them fully into account.

Rates

14. Local rates are a form of taxation, although they also enter into the cost of living, and are necessary to finance the whole range of services to the residents of the area provided by the local authority. Local authorities have been urged to ensure all proper economies in expenditure.

III. INCOMES

15. As explained in paragraph 2, it is the Government's intention that there should be a standstill on all forms of incomes up to the end of 1966, followed by a six-month period of severe restraint.

Employment incomes

16. The standstill to the end of 1966 is intended to apply to increases in pay and to reductions in working hours. It is not proposed that it should be regarded as applying to other conditions of service, except in so far as these are likely to add significantly to labour costs.

17. The term " increases in pay " includes, in addition to basic pay, rates of allowances which are in the nature of pay, rates of pay for overtime and week-end working, piece rates, etc.

18. It is not intended that the standstill should be regarded as applying to—

(i) increases in payments made in specific compensation for expenditure incurred, e.g. travel and subsistence allowances;

(ii) increases in pay resulting directly from increased output, e.g. piece-work earnings, commissions on sales, any necessary increases in overtime worked, profit-sharing schemes, etc.;

(iii) increases in pay genuinely resulting from promotion to work at a higher level, whether with the same or a different employer. (On the other hand, the intention of the standstill would be defeated if employers were to regrade posts as a concealed method of increasing rates of pay);

(iv) it is not intended that the standstill should interfere with the normal arrangements for increasing pay either with age, as with apprentices or juveniles, or by means of regular increments of specified amounts within a predetermined range or scale. Such arrangements are equivalent to promotion according to age or experience. They can thus be distinguished from a commitment to increase pay for a group of employees as a whole, which is affected by the standstill.

Existing commitments

19. At the time of the Prime Minister's statement, at least six million workers—over one worker in four—were expecting an increase in pay or a reduction in hours (or both) during the next twelve months as the result of a long-term agreement or other type of settlement made at some time in the past. It would clearly have been inequitable to introduce a standstill on incomes while allowing these existing commitments to go ahead unchecked. Apart from the unfairness to other workers for whom no such future commitment at present exists, it would in practice have been bound to jeopardise the effectiveness of the standstill from the outset.

20. Although the Government are deeply conscious of the need to restrict to the minimum compatible with the wider economic interests of the country any interference with obligations freely entered into by employers and workers or their representatives, they think it right in the present difficult circumstances to call upon all concerned to accept some deferment. Commitments entered into on or before 20th July 1966 but not yet implemented take a number of different forms:—

(*a*) agreements to increase pay or shorten hours, whether from an operative date before, on or after 20th July 1966;

(*b*) pay increases which may be due under cost-of-living sliding scale arrangements between 20th July 1966 and 30th June 1967;

(*c*) commitments to review pay or hours from a date already agreed on or before 20th July 1966, or standing commitments for periodic review;

(*d*) Wages Council proposals made on or before 20th July 1966 but not yet submitted to the Minister of Labour, or submitted to the Minister but not yet embodied in a statutory order.

21. In all these cases the operative date should be deferred by six months from the original operative date. In those cases in which the original operative date was before 20th July 1966, deferment should be to an operative date six months later, but payment of the increase should not be made before the end of 1966.

22. An existing commitment may be defined as any agreement to increase pay or shorten hours, or any offer to do so, which has been firmly accepted by or on behalf of the workers concerned on or before 20th July 1966.

23. It would clearly defeat the intention of the standstill if the parties concerned were to seek to make good in subsequent negotiations any increases foregone as a result of the standstill. Similarly the deferment of existing commitments necessarily involves the deferment of retrospective dates where these apply.

New Agreements

24. It is not the intention that negotiations should be barred during the standstill period to the end of 1966. But no new agreements entered into after 20th July 1966 should take effect before 1st January 1967 at the earliest, and they should not take effect in the following six months unless they can be justified as falling within the revised criteria referred to in paragraph 25 below.

25. During the six-month period of severe restraint (i.e. the first six months of 1967) the criteria for consideration of new proposals for improvements in pay and hours will be much more stringent than those set out in Part I of the White Paper on Prices and Incomes Policy (Cmnd. 2639), and for the time being the incomes norm must be regarded as zero. The guiding principle must be that of national economic and social priorities. It follows that even in cases which satisfy these more stringent criteria, only limited improvements are likely to be justified during the period of severe restraint. The Government will be consulting the Confederation of British Industry, the Trades Union Congress and other interested parties on the form which these new and stringent criteria should take in order to secure the restraint which the national interest demands.

26. In order that those groups which have an expectation of improvement under commitments already existing should not be treated more severely than those which have not, it will be open to the parties to existing commitments to renegotiate, subject to the standstill, their agreements to take effect during the following six-month period of severe restraint in accordance with the new criteria.

Arbitration

27. Arbitration awards, like settlements negotiated voluntarily, will be subject to the requirements of the periods of standstill and severe restraint.

Other forms of employment income

28. Many individual salaries and other forms of remuneration, including that of company directors and executives, are fixed outside the normal process of collective bargaining; but it is intended that the same principles of standstill and restraint should apply to these as to other forms of income. It is intended to incorporate in a Companies Bill for introduction in the current session of Parliament the statutory requirements relating to disclosure by companies of emoluments of directors and senior executives to which the Prime Minister referred in his statement on 20th July.

29. The scales of charges and fees for self-employed persons, including all forms of professional fees, are expected to be under similar restraint for the twelve months. The Government will have power under the Prices and Incomes Bill to impose a standstill on charges made for professional services.

Other money incomes

30. The Government have already pledged themselves to use their fiscal powers or other means to prevent any excessive growth in aggregate profits.

31. As a result of the Government's fiscal measures, it is not expected that there will be any general increase in dividends during the next twelve months. Nevertheless all company distributions, including dividends paid by companies, are subject to the standstill and should not be increased during the twelve-month period, with the exception of distributions made to meet the requirements of the special tax rates for closely-controlled companies. If there are any cases which, in a company's view, make exemption from the standstill imperative, the company will be expected to inform the Government of the circumstances, in order that the justification may be examined. In important cases the Government will refer the matter to the National Board for Prices and Incomes for examination.

IV. PUBLIC SECTOR

Prices, Charges and Fees of Government Departments

32. The Government intend to apply the principles of the standstill to all prices, charges and fees of Government Departments.

Pay in the public sector

33. Employers and workers in the public services and publicly-owned undertakings will be regarded as under the same obligations to act in accordance with these principles as the rest of the community.

Nationalised Industries

34. The nationalised industries will be subject to the same restraints as the private sector in relation to prices and incomes. They will be subject also to the general provisions of the Prices and Incomes Bill. The Chairmen of the nationalised industries have assured the Government of their full support in

[*63*]

implementing the standstill. The Air Transport Licensing Board, which has before it applications from a number of airlines for increases in fares on domestic air routes, has assured the Government that it will take the Prime Minister's statement of 20th July into account before reaching decisions.

Statutory Price-Fixing Bodies

35. Statutorily established price-fixing bodies, such as the Transport Tribunal or the Traffic Commissioners, are expected to have regard to the principles of the standstill.

V. NATIONAL BOARD FOR PRICES AND INCOMES

36. The Government, the Confederation of British Industry and the Trades Union Congress attach great importance to the continuation of the work of the National Board for Prices and Incomes, both in the longer term and in the special circumstances of the standstill.

37. The fullest use will be made of the Board during the twelve months by referring to it proposals for prices and incomes increases for examination and report. The Board's enquiries will be carried out as rapidly as possible and its organisation will be adapted and strengthened as necessary for this purpose. The parties concerned should defer any increases until the Board has reported and act in the light of the Board's recommendations.

38. The Board will continue during the twelve months to examine references made to it from time to time by the Government on matters of longer term significance in the field of productivity, prices and incomes. This will be of particular importance in preparing for the period following the standstill and period of severe restraint, when it will be essential to ensure that the growth of incomes is resumed in a manner consistent with the growth of national output.

VI. PROPOSED STATUTORY POWERS

39. In his statement on 20th July the Prime Minister said—

"Within the main field of collective bargaining we shall rely in the first instance on voluntary action. Nevertheless, in order to ensure that the selfish do not benefit at the expense of those who co-operate, it is our intention to strengthen the provisions of the Prices and Incomes Bill . . . Meanwhile the Government will not hesitate to act within the powers they enjoy, or may further seek, to deal with any actions involving increases outside and beyond this policy."

40. For this purpose the Government propose to move the addition to the Bill of a new Part containing purely temporary provisions which would be brought into operation by an Order in Council subject to confirmation by both Houses of Parliament within 28 days. Unless previously revoked by Order in Council these powers will lapse automatically 12 months after the Bill receives Royal Assent and cannot be renewed.

41. This new Part will give the Government power to make orders (subject to negative resolution by either House of Parliament) directing that specified

prices or charges, or specified rates of remuneration, shall not be increased from the date of the order without Ministerial consent. A temporary standstill could therefore be imposed where necessary on both prices and charges and on levels of remuneration (allowing for the effect of changes in normal working hours).

42. It will also give power to reverse where necessary unjustified price or pay increases implemented since 20th July 1966. The appropriate Minister could direct that any specified price or charge should be reduced to a level not lower than that prevailing on or before that date. Any such price or charge could not subsequently be raised without Ministerial consent. Before making such a direction, the Minister must give 14 days' advance notice to the person affected by the direction, and must consider any representations made within that time. The direction could not be retrospective. In the case of pay, an order (subject to negative resolution by either House of Parliament) could provide that remuneration of a kind described in the order should be no higher than that paid by the employer for the same kind of work before 20th July 1966, without permission. 14 days' advance notice of the order must be given, and account must be taken of any representations by those concerned.

43. This Part of the Bill will also empower the Ministers concerned to defer the effective dates of wages regulation orders made under the Wages Councils Act and the Agricultural Wages Acts. It will also protect from any legal proceedings employers who, in response to the Government's request for a standstill, voluntarily withhold pay increases to which an employee may be entitled under his contract of employment.

44. As explained above, these powers are temporary. The Prime Minister made it clear in his statement that it was not proposed to introduce elaborate statutory controls over prices and incomes and that the policy must continue to rely on voluntary co-operation. Even though these new powers will be used very selectively, they need to be potentially wide-ranging if they are effectively to deter the selfish minority who are not prepared to co-operate and, no less important, to reassure those who are observing the policy laid down above that they will not be penalised for doing so.

SCHEDULE 3   Sections 9(2) and 23

EXCLUSION FROM SS. 7 AND 8 OF PRICES AND CHARGES
REGULATED UNDER OTHER ENACTMENTS

1. A Minister shall not have power to apply section 7 or 8 of this Act to any price or charge to which this paragraph applies, and any order under the said section 7 or direction under the said section 8 which is so framed as to be capable of referring to such a price or charge shall have effect as if it contained express provision for its exclusion.

2.—(1) The said prices and charges, with the exception of those relating exclusively to Northern Ireland, are as follows:—

(a) pilotage dues within the meaning of the Pilotage Act 1913;

(b) prices for iron and steel products to which section 8 of the Iron and Steel Act 1953 (power of Iron and Steel Board to fix maximum prices) for the time being applies;

[*65*]

(c) charges to which section 6 of the Transport Charges &c. (Miscellaneous Provisions) Act 1954 (power of Minister of Transport to revise charges of certain independent statutory undertakings) for the time being applies;

(d) fares and other charges for carriage, on tramway or other services to which Schedule 1 to the said Act of 1954 applies, where the amount or maximum amount thereof is for the time being governed by any provision of that Schedule;

(e) fares on any service provided under a road service licence granted under the Road Traffic Act 1960, where the amount or maximum amount thereof is for the time being fixed by means of a condition attached to the licence;

(f) charges in respect of any service authorised by an air service licence granted under the Civil Aviation (Licensing) Act 1960, or in respect of any service authorised by a permit granted under an Order in Council made under section 8 of the Civil Aviation Act 1949;

(g) charges with respect to which the Transport Tribunal are empowered to make orders by section 45(1) of the Transport Act 1962;

(h) ship, passenger and goods dues, within the meaning of the Harbours Act 1964, and charges exigible by virtue of section 29 of that Act (local light dues); and

(i) any prices or charges in respect of which, under any local Act, or any provisional order confirmed by Act of Parliament (including any such Act of, or order confirmed by an Act of, the Parliament of Northern Ireland, and Acts and orders passed or confirmed after the commencement of this Act) powers of revision, confirmation or approval are exercisable by any person or body other than the person or body by whom they are charged or made, where the amount or maximum amount thereof is for the time being fixed or authorised in exercise of those powers.

(2) In Northern Ireland, the said prices and charges include also—

(a) charges for the supply of gas by undertakers within the meaning of the Gas Regulation Act 1920; and

(b) charges of harbour authorities which are liable to revision by the Minister of Commerce under the Harbour Authorities (Charges and Borrowing Powers) Act (Northern Ireland) 1956.

3. Nothing in section 7 or 8 of this Act shall prevent any increase in a price or charge which may be necessary to bring it to a minimum amount for the time being required or authorised by any such provision or condition, or in the exercise of any such power, as is mentioned in paragraph 2(1)(d), 2(1)(e) or 2(1)(i) above.

MINISTER
    For meaning, see s. 34 (1), *ante*.

COMMENCEMENT OF THIS ACT
    This Act came into force, in general, on 12th August 1966 (*i.e.*, the date of the Royal Assent) (but as to Parts II and IV, see ss. 6 and 25, *ante*, respectively).

PILOTAGE ACT 1913
By s. 17 (1) (*f*) of that Act (23 Halsbury's Statutes (2nd Edn.) 846), " pilotage dues " means the rates of payments to be made in respect of the services of a licensed pilot.

IRON AND STEEL ACT 1953, S. 8
See 33 Halsbury's Statutes (2nd Edn.) 873.

TRANSPORT CHARGES &C. (MISCELLANEOUS PROVISIONS) ACT 1954, S. 6, SCH. 1
See 34 Halsbury's Statutes (2nd Edn.) 860, 878.

ROAD TRAFFIC ACT 1960
As to road service licences, see ss. 134 *et seq.* of that Act (40 Halsbury's Statutes (2nd Edn.) 830 *et seq.*)

CIVIL AVIATION (LICENSING) ACT 1960
As to air service licences, see ss. 1 *et seq.* of that Act (40 Halsbury's Statutes (2nd Edn.) 27 *et seq.*). So far as this Schedule relates to the Act of 1960 it must be read together with s. 23 (2), (3), *ante.*

CIVIL AVIATION ACT 1949, S. 8
See 28 Halsbury's Statutes (2nd Edn.) 198.

TRANSPORT ACT 1962, S. 45 (1)
See 42 Halsbury's Statutes (2nd Edn.) 607.

HARBOURS ACT 1964
For s. 29 of that Act, see 44 Halsbury's Statutes (2nd Edn.) 1144; and for the meaning of " ship, passenger and goods dues ", see s. 57 (1) of that Act (44 Halsbury's Statutes (2nd Edn.) 1169).

GAS REGULATION ACT 1920
That Act was repealed, except as to Northern Ireland, by the Gas Act 1948, s. 76, Sch. 4 (10 Halsbury's Statutes (2nd Edn.) 954, 977).

HARBOUR AUTHORITIES (CHARGES AND BORROWING POWERS) ACT (NORTHERN IRELAND) 1956
1956 c. 21 (N.I.).

APPENDIX

COMMAND PAPERS ON THE " EARLY-WARNING " SYSTEM
AND THE PRICES AND INCOMES BOARD

MACHINERY OF
PRICES AND INCOMES POLICY

(Cmnd. 2577)

*Presented to Parliament by the First Secretary of State and Secretary of State
for Economic Affairs by Command of Her Majesty, February 1965*

*This memorandum has been prepared by the Government, in agreement with
the Trades Union Congress, the Association of British Chambers of Commerce,
the British Employers' Confederation, the Federation of British Industries and
the National Association of British Manufacturers. It has also been the subject
of discussion by the National Economic Development Council.*

Joint Statement of Intent

1. In the Joint Statement of Intent on Productivity, Prices and Incomes
signed on 16th December, 1964, the representatives of the employers' organisations and the Trades Union Congress undertook on behalf of their members
to co-operate with the Government in endeavouring, in the face of practical
problems, to give effective shape to the machinery that the Government intend
to establish for the following purposes:—

   (i) to keep under review the general movement of prices and of money
   incomes of all kinds;

   (ii) to examine particular cases in order to advise whether or not the
   behaviour of prices or of wages, salaries or other money incomes
   is in the national interest as defined by the Government after consultation with Management and Unions.

Machinery for review

2. The first function involves ascertainment, interpretation and assessment
of the relevant facts about general price and income behaviour. An agreed
policy for prices and incomes requires that representatives of the Government,
Management and Unions should be closely associated with the general review.

It will be appropriate, therefore, to invite the National Economic Development Council to carry out the review.

3. The ascertainment and interpretation of the relevant facts will require considerable statistical and economical expertise as well as complete impartiality. This work will be done by the National Economic Development Office and Government Departments (since most of the factual and statistical material will be provided from Government sources) and the results embodied in reports submitted by the National Economic Development Office to the National Economic Development Council.

4. The National Economic Development Council will review the reports submitted to it and consider their implications for the national interest. In the light of this review, Government, Management and Unions will be expected to take any action that may be required in their respective spheres of responsibility.

Machinery to examine particular cases

5. The Government have discussed with Management and Unions the practical problems involved in establishing machinery to investigate particular cases of price and income behaviour and with their agreement now propose the setting up under Royal Warrant of a National Board for Prices and Incomes working in two separate divisions, to be known as the Prices Review Division and the Incomes Review Division respectively.

6. The Government have been encouraged by the Statement of Intent and in subsequent discussions to believe that all the parties concerned will give the Board their voluntary co-operation in its investigations of particular cases. The Government would have to consider giving the Board statutory authority, however, if experience showed this was necessary.

Composition

7. The Board will consist of an independent Chairman, a number of independent members, a businessman and a trade unionist. Some of the members may be part-time. Collectively, the independent members will need to have expertise in law, accountancy, economics, industrial relations and other relevant fields. In addition to these permanent appointments to the Board, panels of businessmen and trade unionists will be appointed to assist the Prices Review Division and the Incomes Review Division with the investigation of particular cases.

8. Two of the full-time independent members will share with the Chairman of the Board the chairmanship of the Prices Review Division and the Incomes Review Division. Each Division will be enabled to sit in two or more sections under an independent chairman. The Chairman of the Board will be responsible for allocating work to the Divisions and between sections of each Division, as well as for co-ordinating the work of the two Divisions.

Staff

9. The Board will have its own staff, which will include accountants, experts on industrial relations, economists and statisticians.

The Prices Review Division
Cases to be investigated

10. The success of the prices policy will depend on the extent to which individual firms apply it in practice. There will also have to be a willingness to accept investigation of individual cases referred to the Prices Review Division. The national employers' organisations and the T.U.C. will have a vital part to play in securing the support of their members for the policy. It will also be helpful if the national employers' organisations can advise their members on the application of the policy.

11. In principle, the Prices Review Division will be able to investigate any price or group of prices (manufacturing, wholesale or retail) of goods and services in private industry and in nationalised industry. Both particular cases of price changes and cases in which there has been no change, although prima facie some reduction appears to be warranted, will be covered.

Procedure for making references

12. The Government will retain direct responsibility for all references to the Prices Review Division. Some of these may result from complaints made to the Government by individuals, interested parties or independent bodies; others will be directly selected by the Government as meriting detailed investigation.

Procedure and speed of investigation

13. The Division will decide its own procedure, and in particular how far, if at all, it will sit in public. The Division will no doubt take evidence from the industry or firms whose prices are under examination, and from any other interested party (e.g. representatives of purchasers or consumers). Any evidence of a confidential nature, the publication of which would damage the legitimate business interests of the firm concerned, will be taken in private and will not be published. Two to three months should be the maximum for the length of an inquiry.

Incomes Review Division
Cases to be investigated

14. The success of the policy will depend on the extent to which unions and employers and others concerned with fixing incomes apply it in practice. There will also have to be a willingness on the part of those directly concerned to accept investigation of claims, settlements and other questions relating to incomes referred to the Incomes Review Division. The T.U.C. and B.E.C. (or Confederation of British Industry) will have a vital part to play in securing the support of their members for the policy. It will also be helpful if they can advise their members on the application of the policy.

15. In principle it will be desirable for the Division to be able to investigate claims and settlements relating to wage and salary increases, reductions in hours and other improvements in conditions of service, whether in the private sector, the nationalised industries or the public services; cases in which a revaluation of pay levels or an overhaul of the pay structure seems to be indicated for economic or social reasons; the level of earnings in an industry

or sector; and, where appropriate, cases of increases in money incomes other than wages and salaries.

Procedure for making references

16. As in the case of prices, the Government will retain direct responsibility for all references of claims, settlements and other questions to the Incomes Review Division. Some of these may be at the request of one or both parties, others may be directly selected by the Government as meriting investigation. It is hoped that in all cases the parties directly concerned will be willing to have claims brought before the Division where the Government consider this is desirable in the national interest.

Procedure and speed of investigation

17. The Incomes Review Division, like the Prices Review Division, will decide its own procedure, including the extent to which it will sit in public. It will no doubt take evidence from the parties immediately concerned and from other interested parties. Reports should be available within two or three months of references being made, and if possible even more quickly in the case of claims.

Acceptance of Board's findings and recommendations

18. The Government intend to give the voluntary method every chance of proving that it can be made to work. Accordingly, in the case of both prices and incomes, persuasion and the pressure of public opinion will be relied upon to ensure that the findings and recommendations of the Board are accepted by the parties concerned. The Government would resort to other methods only if they were convinced that the voluntary method had failed.

PRICES AND INCOMES POLICY

(Cmnd. 2639)

Presented to Parliament by the First Secretary of State and Secretary of State for Economic Affairs by Command of Her Majesty, April 1965

This Command Paper may be regarded as obsolete. It consisted of two parts. Part I (general considerations relating to prices and incomes) was reproduced in Sch. 2 to the Prices and Incomes Act 1966 (see s. 4 (1) thereof). Certain comments thereon are to be found in §§ 17-23. The Secretary of State has, however, substituted, by order under s. 4 (2), a new Sch. 2, which reproduces the White Paper of July 1966, " Prices and Incomes Standstill " (Cmnd. 3073). Part II (the National Board for Prices and Incomes) is superseded by provisions of Part I of the Act.

PRICES AND INCOMES POLICY :
AN " EARLY WARNING " SYSTEM

(Cmnd. 2808)

*Presented to Parliament by the First Secretary of State and Secretary of State
for Economic Affairs by Command of Her Majesty, November 1965*

Introduction

The Government announced on 2nd September 1965 their intention to
seek statutory power to introduce a compulsory " early warning " system for
prices and incomes, i.e. to take power to require advance notification to the
Government of an intended increase in prices or charges, of claims relating to
pay, hours or other major improvements; and of prospective terms of
settlement in such cases. Some delay is inevitable before legislation can be
enacted for this purpose; and the Government have in any case undertaken
to consult the Trades Union Congress and the Confederation of British
Industry further before bringing statutory provisions of this nature into
effect. It is accordingly important that an " early warning " system should be
introduced on a non-statutory basis as soon as possible. The proposed
arrangements for such a non-statutory scheme are described in the following
paragraphs; they have been drawn up in discussion with the Trades Union
Congress and the Confederation of British Industry.

Purpose of advance notification

2. The purpose of an " early warning " system for price increases and for
increases in pay, reductions in hours or other major improvements is to give
the Government an adequate opportunity to consider decisions concerning
prices and pay before they are put into effect. Such advance warning is
important if the agreed policy for productivity, prices and incomes is to work
effectively. For example, the question whether a particular case should or
should not be referred to the National Board for Prices and Incomes requires
careful consideration of the relevant facts. It would be unsatisfactory for such
review to be undertaken without knowledge of the facts or in undue haste.
Moreover it would be unfair if the policy were in practice to impinge more
heavily on those whose intentions were known in advance than on those who
kept their plans to themselves.

Prices
Goods and services covered

3. Although the agreed policy for prices and incomes applies with equal
force to all who are responsible for determining prices and charges, it is
neither necessary nor practicable to have " early warning " of each of the
very large number of individual price changes which are liable to occur in the
course of a year. In general the aim must be to include goods and services
which are of particular economic significance, or consumer goods which are
important elements in the cost of living. In drawing up a list, however, it is

necessary to have regard to factors which make inclusion of particular items unsuitable. Examples of these are goods the prices of which are determined by very short term supply and demand factors or mainly by the cost of imported materials.

4. The consumer goods to be included should be of general consumer interest and reasonably representative of this class of goods: they should also present fewer difficulties of administration than other items which have been considered. For example, some goods such as clothing present great difficulties because the product is both varied and is continually changing or because a very large number of small firms are involved. Industrial goods which are frequently designed to meet particular needs or which tend to be sold on the basis of individually negotiated contracts rather than of standard prices have been omitted, as also have items where an important part of the supply does not enter into price transactions in the normal way.

5. Because of the importance of food to the cost of living the Government feel that close attention must be paid to all food prices. A wide range of products, representing just over half of all consumer expenditure on food and drink, will be subject to the " early warning " arrangements. But these arrangements cannot be applied to a number of important commodities, mainly primary products, the prices of which are so largely influenced by short-term market factors that it is impracticable to give advance notice of price increases. The prices of these commodities will continue to be subject to constant watch by the Ministry of Agriculture, Fisheries and Food. In addition, the Government directly control the price of milk. In this way the whole range of food prices will be covered.

6. In the light of the considerations discussed above it is proposed that the goods and services for which advance notification can most appropriately be requested are those listed in Part A of the Appendix. In applying the general arrangements to individual items the Government will consult the various industries concerned. For example, problems of definition are likely to arise, and in some cases it will be desirable for practical reasons to ensure that the arrangements do not create an excessive burden of additional work in relation to the objectives described above. The Government Departments concerned will be consulting the various industries (through trade associations or other appropriate channels) on questions of this sort without delay. The list is provisional. It will be reviewed later in the light of experience, and may be amended from time to time in consultation with the industries concerned.

7. The foodstuffs subject to constant watch, as described in paragraph 5, are listed in Part B of the Appendix. Certain other prices and charges are subject to regulation by independent statutory authorities and for this reason need not be covered by a non-statutory " early warning " system. The more important of these are shown in Part C of the Appendix.

Type of price covered

8. The arrangements will apply primarily to manufacturers' prices and only to manufacturers' prices for the home market. In some cases it may be more appropriate to cover wholesale or retail prices, for example where the

manufacturer is also the retailer. It is not normally intended to cover prices which are fixed by individual contract or some similar process.

Action to be taken by manufacturers, etc.

9. Any enterprise which plans to increase the price of any of the goods and services listed in Part A of the Appendix is asked to inform the appropriate Government Department not less than four weeks before the date from which the price increase is to take effect. In general the following information should be provided, together with a brief assessment of the justification for the proposed increase in the light of the considerations set out in the White Paper on Prices and Incomes Policy (Cmnd. 2639): a description of the goods or services concerned, including any changes being made in the product or in the service offered, the present price and the proposed price and the price trend over the previous three years, the annual sales value of the goods or services concerned, the reason for the price increase and, where this is due to cost increases, an explanation of these together with a statement of the part played in total costs by e.g. labour, raw materials and other costs. Detailed requirements will be discussed with individual industries.

Action by the Government

10. On receipt of advance notification the Government Departments concerned will consider whether further enquiries are desirable and if so will communicate with the firm. The object of such enquiries will be to enable the Government to form a judgment whether the proposed price increase would be consistent with the agreed principles set out in Cmnd. 2639 and whether there is a prima facie case for reference of the case to the National Board for Prices and Incomes. It will not be the object of the Departmental enquiries at this stage to undertake a detailed examination comparable with that which might be undertaken by the National Board for Prices and Incomes.

Nationalised industries and Government Departments

11. The nationalised industries and Government Departments will be covered by the proposed arrangements in the same way as private industry. Separate guidance will be issued for this purpose.

Standstill period

12. In the absence of any indication by the Government to the contrary before the end of the four-week period, the enterprise will be entitled to assume that the Government have decided to take no action, though this will not imply any positive approval or endorsement by the Government of the change. But in cases where the Government indicate that they see a need for more prolonged enquiry or for reference of the case to the National Board for Prices and Incomes, the enterprise will be expected to defer introduction of the price change until the further enquiry has been undertaken or the Board has reported. The period of decision for the Government will normally be less than 28 days. The Board will be expected to report at the earliest possible date and where speed is more than usually important this will be drawn to the Board's notice in the reference. The object will be to ensure that the total

standstill period, including the period between the original notification and the formal reference to the Board, does not exceed three months.

Confidential nature of information

13. Any information which the Government receive under these arrangements will be treated as confidential (although reference to the National Board for Prices and Incomes will be announced publicly as hitherto).

Pay and Conditions of Employment

14. In the field of pay, hours, etc. the Government will require information about claims, the progress of negotiations and terms of settlement. The information about claims should specify the nature of the claim, the number and category of workers covered and the date and terms of the previous settlement covering this group of workers. Where information is required about terms of settlement it should include a brief assessment of the justification for the proposed improvement in the light of the considerations set out in Cmnd. 2639.

15. If the policy is not to weigh more heavily on some groups of workers than on others, information is required relating not only to national negotiations but also to negotiations at local and company level. However, for practical reasons it will be necessary to exclude from the " early warning " system claims which, because of the small number of workers involved or for other reasons, are of relatively little significance. It is intended to review this matter in the light of the experience of the Trades Union Congress and the Confederation of British Industry in operating their arrangements for notification.

Action by the Trades Union Congress

16. In accordance with the decision taken at the recent Congress, the Trades Union Congress has introduced arrangements whereby the General Council is informed by affiliated unions of all impending claims. These claims are examined by a special committee established for this purpose, consisting of one General Council member from each of the 19 Trade Groups of Congress.

17. Where the General Council does not wish to make any comment on the claim, the union will be informed within about a month of receipt of the claim by the Trades Union Congress. In some cases the General Council may wish to make written observations on the claim or to invite representatives of the union or unions concerned to meet them to discuss it. In the latter event, the meeting will be arranged as quickly as possible after the committee has considered the claim. In the great majority of cases, not more than five weeks or so at the most should elapse between receipt of the notification and completion of the procedure. Until then unions will be expected to refrain from proceeding with the claim but thereafter they will be free to proceed, taking account of such considerations as the General Council may draw to their attention.

18. The Trades Union Congress will keep the Government informed of developments, with the object of meeting the Government's " early warning " requirements in respect of affiliated unions.

Action by non-affiliated unions

19. Unions and staff associations, etc. not affiliated to the Trades Union Congress will be expected to follow the same procedure, except that notification of all claims should be to the Ministry of Labour* and the Ministry should be kept informed of major developments during the course of negotiations. The information provided should be on the lines indicated in paragraph 14 above.

Action by the Confederation of British Industry

20. The Confederation of British Industry is arranging to provide the Government with information about claims, formal offers, references to arbitration and terms of settlement reported by their members. So far as national claims and settlements are concerned, the Confederation of British Industry will itself collect the information and pass it on to the Ministry of Labour. Information about local and company negotiations will be supplied to the Ministry of Labour* direct by the firms and employers' organisations concerned. Initially, for practical reasons, the Confederation of British Industry are requesting their members to give information in respect only of negotiations affecting more than 1,000 workers.

Action by other employers

21. Employers' organisations which are not members of the Confederation of British Industry, and firms which are neither members of the Confederation of British Industry nor members of member employers' organisations, will be expected similarly to supply information about claims, formal offers and terms of settlement direct to the Ministry of Labour*. The information should be on the lines indicated in paragraph 14 above.

Public sector

22. Similar arrangements are being introduced in respect of pay claims relating to the Civil Service, the National Health Service and other public services, and the nationalised industries. Detailed arrangements will be drawn up in consultation with the various organisations concerned.

Action by the Government

23. On receipt of advance information under these arrangements the Government Departments concerned will consider whether further enquiries are desirable and, if so, will communicate with the negotiating parties. The object of these enquiries will be to enable the Government to judge whether the settlement of the claim is likely to be consistent with the principles laid down in Cmnd. 2639 and whether there is a prima facie case for reference to the National Board for Prices and Incomes. In general it will be desirable to refer a claim, where this course is judged to be in the national interest, at as early a stage of the negotiations as possible. Although the Government will have power to refer any claim or settlement to the Board, priority will in most cases have to be given to claims which are of particular economic or social significance.

---

* Notification should be made to the Ministry of Labour, Industrial Relations Department (I.R.A.8), 8 St. James's Square, London, S.W.1.

Confidential nature of information

24. Any information which the Government receive under these arrangements will be treated as confidential (although references to the National Board for Prices and Incomes will be announced publicly as hitherto).

Standstill period

25. In cases in which the Government indicate that there is a need for reference to the National Board for Prices and Incomes, the parties will be expected to suspend further action until the Board has reported. It is expected that the Board will normally report within two to three months. Where speed is more than usually important this will be drawn to the Board's notice in the reference.

Principles of the White Paper on Prices and Incomes Policy (Cmnd. 2639)

26. It must be emphasised that the new arrangements described above in no way relieve those concerned with determining prices and incomes of the obligation to act in accordance with the principles set out in Cmnd. 2639. To keep the general level of prices stable, it is vital that price increases should be avoided where possible and that prices should be reduced wherever circumstances permit; and that the overall increase in wages, salaries and other forms of incomes should be kept in line with the growth of real national output. The Government are free to refer appropriate cases to the National Board for Prices and Incomes whether or not they are subject to the " early warning " system.

APPENDIX

PART A

PROVISIONAL LIST OF GOODS AND SERVICES SUBJECT TO " EARLY WARNING "

Bread
Flour
Biscuits
Cakes
Breakfast cereals
Sausages
Meat pies
Canned meats
Canned fish
Quick-frozen fish
Margarine
Lard and compound fats
Jams and marmalade
Chocolate and sugar confectionery
Condensed milk
Canned fruit
Canned vegetables
Quick-frozen vegetables
Processed vegetables

Notification to:
The Assistant Secretary,
Ministry of Agriculture, Fisheries and
Food,
Prices Branch,
Whitehall Place (West Block),
*London, S.W.*1.
Telephone: TRAfalgar 7711.

PART A—*continued*

Notification to:

Pickles and sauces
Soft drinks
Ice-cream
Tea
Processed coffee
Spirits
Beer

The Assistant Secretary,
Ministry of Agriculture, Fisheries and
Food,
Prices Branch,
Whitehall Place (West Block),
London, S.W.1.
Telephone: TRAfalgar 7711

Notification to:

Electric motors
Primary cells and primary batteries
Secondary batteries
Precision chains
Ball and roller bearings
Contractors' plant
Agricultural machinery
Tractors
Commercial vehicles
Motor cars
Bicycles and motor cycles
Perambulators
Tyres
Domestic refrigerators
Gas cookers
Electric cookers
Washing machines
Vacuum cleaners
Electric fires
Gas fires
Electric storage heaters
Domestic boilers
Domestic water heaters
Electric lamps—coil and fluorescent
Cash registers
Typewriters
Domestic sewing machines
Industrial sewing machines
Synthetic sole sheeting
Upper leather, sole leather and cut soles
Rubber footwear
Textile yarn and thread and man-made
    staple fibre
Paper and board
Wallpaper
National daily and Sunday newspapers
Oxygen and acetylene
P.V.C. and polyethylene
Nitrogenous fertilisers
Household soaps and detergents
Glass jars and bottles

The Assistant Secretary,
Board of Trade,
1, Victoria Street,
London, S.W.1.
Telephone: ABBey 7877.

PART A—*continued*

Radio and television sets

Notification to:
The Assistant Secretary,
Ministry of Technology,
L Branch,
Millbank Tower,
Millbank, London, S.W.1.
Telephone: VICtoria 2255.

Bricks
Cement
Glass
Sand and gravel
Plasterboard

Notification to:
The Director of Economic Intelligence,
Ministry of Public Building and Works,
Lambeth Bridge House,
London, S.E.1.
Telephone: RELiance 7611.

Petrol
Derv
Fuel oils

Notification to:
The Assistant Secretary,
Ministry of Power,
Petroleum Division,
Thames House South,
Millbank, London, S.W.1.
Telephone: ABBey 7000.

*Coal
*Coke
*Manufactured fuel
*Gas
*Electricity (England and Wales)
*Electricity (Scotland)

Notification to:
As at present.

†Rail fares (outside London Passenger
    Transport Area)
†Rail freight charges
†British Road Services charges (parcels)

Notification to:
As at present.

PART B

FOOD PRICES UNDER CONSTANT WATCH BY THE MINISTRY OF AGRICULTURE, FISHERIES AND FOOD

Carcase meat and offal
Bacon
Poultry (including broilers)
Eggs
Fresh fruit
Fresh vegetables (including potatoes)
Fish
Sugar
Cheese
Butter

---

*Subject also to the procedures of consulting statutory consumers' councils.
†Notifications will be confined to country-wide changes in fares and charges generally, and changes in published scales for parcels and sundries.

PART C

PRICES AND CHARGES SUBJECT TO REGULATION BY INDEPENDENT STATUTORY AUTHORITIES

Iron and steel products, as defined in the Iron and Steel Act, 1953

Passenger fares of the London Transport Board and railways in the London area

Other bus fares

Internal air fares (scheduled passenger services)

Ship, passenger and goods dues, as defined in the Harbours Act, 1964.

INDEX

§ indicates a paragraph of the narrative text (pages 1—53).
s. indicates a section of the Act (pages [1]—[50].
Sch. indicates a Schedule to the Act (pages [51]—[67].
Cmnd. indicates a Command Paper (pages [69]—[81].

A

AGREEMENT,
conditional sale, price restriction, § 179, s. 34
hire-purchase, price restriction, § 179, s. 34
pay and hours, on, negotiations during standstill, § 38, Sch. 2, paras. 24–26
    deferment, § 37, s. 30, Sch. 2, paras. 19–23
productivity, restraint on implementation, § 67
Restrictive Trade Practices Act, 1956, under, approved, exception for, s. 24
    meaning, s. 24

AGRICULTURAL WAGES,
increase, deferment of, §§ 58, 85, s. 32

AIR TRANSPORT LICENSING BOARD,
principles to be applied by, s. 23, Sch. 2

AIRCRAFT,
British, pay increases, restrictions on, s. 28

APPEALS, § 12

APPRENTICE,
wage scale, whether affected by standstill, §§ 36, 88, Sch. 2, para. 18

ARBITRATION AWARD,
wages, on, standstill on implementation, Sch. 2, para. 27

ATTORNEY GENERAL,
consent to proceedings, § 174, s. 22

AUCTION,
sale by, exception from standstill, §§ 68, 72, 121, ss. 9, 26, 27

AWARDS AND SETTLEMENTS. *See* Wages

B

BASIS YEAR,
limited company, of, how established, § 133, s. 12

BELFAST GAZETTE. *See* Gazette

BOARD FOR PRICES AND INCOMES. *See* National Board for Prices and
Incomes

BUILDING SOCIETIES,
period of restraint, position under, §§ 190, 191

BUSINESS,
meaning, § 169, s. 34

Index

C

CAPITAL,
company, of, adjustment for determination of dividend increase, §§ 141–143, s. 12

CHARGES,
comparison, how made, § 124, s. 10
domestic air services, on, s. 23; Sch. 2
early warning system. *See* EARLY WARNING SYSTEM
fares, exceptions from restrictions, Sch. 3, para. 2
increase, discounts, how treated, § 113, s. 26
    how determined, §§ 66, 67, 124, ss. 10, 25, 26
    meaning, § 171, s. 11
    minimum, to bring up to, Sch. 3, para. 3
    restrictions on, §§ 68–70, s. 26
    unauthorised, offences and penalties, §§ 70, 125, 174, 175, ss. 11, 26, 27
        proceedings, defences to, § 125, s. 11
        recovery by customer, § 70, s. 9
levels at July 20, 1966, restriction to §§ 71–74, s. 27
National Board, reference to. *See* NATIONAL BOARD FOR PRICES AND INCOMES
standstill. *See* STANDSTILL

CIVIL AVIATION (LICENSING) ACT, 1960,
domestic air fares, principles to be applied, s. 23; Sch. 3, para. 2

CLOSE COMPANIES,
distribution, restraint on, exceptions to, § 139, Sch. 2, para. 31

COLLECTIVE BARGAINS,
enforcement of, § 82

COMMISSION ON SALES,
exception from standstill, § 36, Sch. 2, para. 18

COMPANY,
director. *See* DIRECTOR OF COMPANY
distributions, increase, close companies, § 40, Sch. 2, para. 31
    method of ascertainment, §§ 133–135, s. 12
    notice of, §§ 136–138, s. 12
    offences and penalties, §§ 138, 175, s. 12
  meaning, §§ 139, 140, s. 12
  order applying Act to, § 128, s. 12
  relevant decision, meaning, §§ 144–146, s. 12
  share capital issued, adjustment by, §§ 141–143, s. 12
  standstill, whether applicable to, § 127, s. 12
financial year, basis, meaning, § 133, s. 12
    order prescribing, §§ 133–135, s. 12
    meaning, s. 12
inquiry, offences as to, Sch. 1, para. 14
meaning, s. 12
officers of, personal liability, § 175, s. 22
secretary, personal liability, § 175, s. 22
share capital. *See* SHARE CAPITAL

CONDITIONAL SALE,
price restriction, application to, § 179, s. 34

CONFEDERATION OF BRITISH INDUSTRY,
early warning system, participation in, §§ 8, 24; Cmnd. 2808, para. 20

CONTRACT OF EMPLOYMENT,
increase of wages due under, authority to disregard, §§ 81, 82, s. 30
rescission by employee, retention of right of, s. 30
United Kingdom, to be performed outside, exception for, s. 30

CORPORATION. *See also* CORPORATION
officers of, personal liability, § 175, s. 22

COST-OF-LIVING SCALES,
invalidation during restraint, § 88

CROWN,
employment under, application of standstill to, §§ 76, 166, ss. 18, 28
national health service employees regarded as employed by, § 166, s. 18
Northern Ireland, in right of Government of, s. 18
obligations of employer, whether binding on, §§ 76, 166, ss. 18, 28

D

DEFINITIONS,
appropriate Minister, §§ 167, 178, s. 34
awards and settlements, § 168, s. 34
basis financial year, § 133, s. 12
business, § 169, s. 34
company, s. 12
director, s. 12
of nationalised industry, s. 22
distribution, § 139, s. 12
employee, s. 34
financial year, §§ 133–135, s. 12
Gazette, § 173, s. 34
goods, § 170, s. 34
normal working hours, s. 25
preference dividend, s. 12
price, § 171, s. 34
public notice, § 172, s. 34
share, s. 12
capital, s. 12
trade association, s. 34
dispute, § 165, s. 17
union, s. 34

DIRECTOR OF COMPANY,
disclosure of emoluments, § 180, Sch. 2, para. 28
meaning, s. 12
offences, personal liability, § 175, s. 22

DISCLOSURE,
inquiry, at, powers to require, § 99, Sch. 1, para. 14
wrongful, penalties for, § 100, Sch. 1, para. 16

DISCOUNT,
standstill on prices and charges, allowance for, §§ 68, 113, ss. 7, 26

DIVIDENDS,
distribution. *See under* COMPANY
preference, assumption as to payment, s. 12
meaning, s. 12

Index

E

EARLY WARNING SYSTEM. *And see under* STANDSTILL
Confederation of British Industry, participation in, §§ 8, 24; Cmnd. 2808, para. 20
goods and services subject to, § 25, Cmnd. 2808, Appendix A
pay and conditions of employment, claims, notice of, § 28, Cmnd. 2808, paras. 14, 15
    Confederation of British Industry, action by, § 24, Cmnd. 2808, para. 20
    confidential nature of information, Cmnd. 2808, para. 24
    employers' organisations, duties under, Cmnd. 2808, para. 21
    Government, action by, § 24, Cmnd. 2808, para. 23
    non-affiliated unions, action by, Cmnd. 2808, para. 19
    public sector, in, §§ 41, 42, Cmnd. 2808, para. 22
    standstill period, Cmnd. 2808, para. 25
    Trades Union Congress, action by, § 24, Cmnd. 2808, paras. 16–18
prices and charges, confidential nature of information, Cmnd. 2808, para. 13
    food stuffs, watch by Ministry, § 26, Cmnd. 2808, Appendix B
    goods and services covered, § 25, Cmnd. 2808, paras. 3–7
    Government, action by, § 24, Cmnd. 2808, para. 10
    departments, § 25, Cmnd. 2808, para. 11
    independent statutory authorities, subject to regulation by, Cmnd. 2808, Appendix C
    manufacturers, action to be taken by, Cmnd. 2808, para. 9
    nationalised industries, Cmnd. 2808, para. 11
    standstill period, during, § 31, Cmnd. 2808, para. 12
    type covered by, § 25, Cmnd. 2808, para. 8
purpose of, § 24, Cmnd. 2808, para. 2
Trades Union Congress, participation in, §§ 7, 24; Cmnd. 2808, paras. 16–18

EDINBURGH GAZETTE. *See* GAZETTE

EMPLOYEE,
meaning, s. 34

EMPLOYER,
awards and settlements, duty to notify, § 149, s. 14
    offences and penalties, § 151, ss. 14, 16
Crown as. *See* CROWN
pay claim, duty to notify, §§ 150–152, s. 13
    increase, making unauthorised, offences and penalties, §§ 174–176, s. 28
terms and conditions of employment, offences as to, §§ 151, 174–176, s. 16
wages, unauthorised payments, inability to recover, § 79, s. 33
    offences and penalties, §§ 80, 163, 174–176, ss. 16, 29

EMPLOYERS' ORGANISATION,
offences by, proceedings for, § 174, s. 22

EMPLOYMENT,
Contract of. *See* CONTRACT OF EMPLOYMENT
Crown, under. *See* CROWN
terms and conditions, standstill on, §§ 75–85, 149–166, ss. 13–18, 28–32
wages. *See* WAGES

Index

EXPORT TRADE,
standstill on prices, exception from, § 118, s. 9

F

FALSE STATEMENT,
inquiry, at, Sch. 1, para. 14

FARES,
domestic air services, on, application of principles, § 57, s. 23; Sch. 2
exceptions from restrictions, Sch. 3, para. 2

FINANCIAL YEAR OF COMPANY,
basis, meaning, § 133, s. 12
    order prescribing, § 134, s. 12
meaning, s. 13

" FREEZE ". *See* PRICES; STANDSTILL; WAGES

FRINGE BENEFITS, §§ 66, 149

G

GAZETTE,
awards and settlements, receipt of notice of, notification in, § 101, s. 14
continuous review of prices or incomes, instructions to maintain, publication in
    § 103, s. 3
intention to increase prices or charges, reference to Board, publication of,
    § 101, s. 7
meaning, § 173, s. 34
order restricting pay, notice of, publication in, § 180, s. 29
questions referred to Board, publication in, § 101, s. 2
report by Board, announcement in, § 106, s. 5

GOVERNMENT DEPARTMENT,
early warning system, application to, § 25, Cmnd. 2808, para. 11
expenses, defrayment of, s. 35

H

HARBOURS,
dues, exception from restrictions, Sch. 3, para. 2

HIRE PURCHASE,
price restriction, application to, § 179, s. 34

HOUSE OF COMMONS DISQUALIFICATION ACT, 1957,
members of Prices and Incomes Board, application to, § 92, Sch. 1, para. 4

I

IN CAMERA,
inquiry by Board, powers to hold, Sch. 1, para. 13

INCOMES,
dividends, from. *See* COMPANY
National Board. *See* NATIONAL BOARD FOR PRICES AND INCOMES
self-employment, from, considerations affecting, §§ 39, 40, 180, 181, Sch. 2,
    para. 29
wages. *See* WAGES

INFORMATION,
inquiry, at, powers to require, § 99, Sch. 1, para. 14
    wrongful disclosure, § 100, Sch. 1, para. 16

University of Ottawa
Social Sciences Sociales

T

Index

TRADE DISPUTE. *See also* STRIKE
extended meaning, § 75, s. 17

TRADE UNION,
awards and settlement, notification, responsibility for, § 151, s. 14
documents, service on, § 174, s. 22
fine, funds from which payable, § 174, s. 22
inquiry, offences in connection with, Sch. 1, para. 14
meaning, § 167, s. 34
offences by, proceedings for, § 174, s. 22
pay claims, notice of, responsibility for, § 151, s. 13
strike to enforce award or settlement, inducing, §§ 75, 165, s. 16
trade dispute, extended meaning, § 75, s. 17

TRADES UNION CONGRESS,
early warning system, participation in, § 7; Cmnd. 2808, paras. 16–18

VOCATION,
included in business, § 169, s. 34

W

WAGES,
arbitration award, standstill on, § 161, Sch. 2, para. 27
awards and settlements, application of early warning system, §§ 149, 154–164,
s. 14
employer, duty to notify, § 155, s. 14
implementation, permitted, when, § 159, s. 15
unauthorised, penalties, § 161, s. 16
meaning, § 168, s. 34
notice of, Gazette, notification in, § 156, s. 14
order, coming into force before, § 158, s. 14
standstill on, order imposing, § 159, s. 15
strike to enforce implementation, penalties for, § 165,
s. 16
commitments on wages or hours, deferment of, §§ 81, 82, Sch. 2, paras. 19–23
cost-of-living scales, invalidation of, § 88
early warning system, pay claims, descriptions, distinctions in, § 150, s. 13
notice of, approval of organisation giving,
§ 151, s. 13
responsibility for giving, § 151,
s. 13
powers to make compulsory, § 154, s. 13;
Cmnd. 2808, paras. 14, 15
presented before coming into force of order,
§ 152, s. 13
increase, authority for payment, §§ 75, 80, ss. 28, 29
existing contract, under, authority to disregard, §§ 81, 82, s. 30
how determined, § 66, s. 25
improved output, whether justified by, § 88
meaning, § 35
order restricting, powers to give, § 75, s. 28
publication in Gazette, § 80, s. 29
representations against, § 80, s. 29
unauthorised, offences and penalties, § 80, s. 29
Wages Councils Act, 1959, suspension of certain provisions, § 83, s. 31
National Board, review by. *See* NATIONAL BOARD FOR PRICES AND INCOMES
normal working hours, meaning, s. 25
remuneration for work outside, how considered,
§ 36, s. 25

[*94*]

WAGES—*cont.*
over-time payments, how affected, § 36, Sch. 2, para. 18
piece-work exception from standstill, § 36, Sch. 2, para. 18
promotion, increase resulting from, § 36, Sch. 2, para. 18
scale, predetermined, increments within, §§ 36, 79, Sch. 2, para. 18
standstill on, early warning system, under, § 159, ss. 13–18; Cmnd. 2808, paras. 25
    restraint from July 20, 1966, §§ 75–85, ss. 28–32; Sch. 2, paras. 15–29
wage-regulation orders, relief from duty to make, §§ 83, 84, s. 31
    proposals, power to postpone, §§ 83, 84, s. 31

WAGES COUNCILS ACT, 1959
suspension of certain provisions, § 83, s. 31

WHOLESALER,
price standstill, application to, Sch. 2, para. 7

WITNESS AT INQUIRY. *See* INQUIRIES

Université d Ottawa
Social Sciences Sociales

6015 6 — 310